Developing Your Sales Team

The Essential Sales Playbook for Founders and Entrepreneurial CEOs

Steve Kraner

ISBN: 9781095149737

This book is dedicated to my dear wife, Judy Elias Kraner, who, along with being a wonderful friend and Mother, is also a brilliant business partner and confidante.

ACKNOWLEDGMENTS

Thanks to those daring and intrepid men and women who build new companies from the ground up to meet the needs of an ever more complex global marketplace. I am grateful for the inspiration they provide me every day. I hope I can provide just a little sustenance along the way, and perhaps prevent a few avoidable headaches.

ABOUT THE AUTHOR

Steve Kraner is NOT a natural salesman. He describes himself as an engineer who crossed over to the dark side. He holds a Bachelor's Degree in Engineering from West Point and an MBA from Loyola College. He has built successful high-tech divisions within two major U.S. corporations. His experience includes winning in commercial and federal selling environments.

Steve entertains as he enlightens. He combines colorful personal experiences to give you a fresh, unflinching perspective on the sales process. His unique brand of sales edutainment is generously spiced with humorous, real-world stories garnered during a colorful, 17-year sales and sales management career. He invites audiences to challenge him, and the highlight of his programs is the "no-holds-barred" interaction that results.

Your team will buy in to Steve's innovative and dogma-shattering approach to selling because it's clearly not theory, but real-world strategy and tactics that he personally uses to sell. Steve's clients include fast growth companies like Google, Black Duck Software, Synopsys, Risk Lens, Recorded Future, Salesforce, Logi Analytics, WeddingWire, Tenable Network Security, Imprivata, Deque Systems, and industry thoroughbreds like IBM, Cisco Systems, Oracle, and McAfee Software.

An entrepreneur's success starts with a novel product or service, but early stage CEO's often have a "field of dreams" mentality; if they build it customers will come. But defining the offering is only part of getting launched. Entrepreneurs must also think about the sales process to achieve success.

CONTENTS

FOREWORD

Crossing over to the dark side

I was an engineer who could never have imagined myself as a salesperson. I had turned down sales jobs even though the pay was better. Being a salesperson was inconceivable to me. Until one day my engineering career led me to a role as the engineering manager in a startup organization within the company I was working for. I was the third person hired.

Because the startup was internal, we were dependent on the sales force of the larger corporate entity, which was infamously weak and undependable. I was forced to sell just so my group would survive. I crossed from engineering to sales. I now spent most of my time bringing in business. I had crossed over to the dark side.

Once I began to sell, however, I realized that selling was not at all what I thought it was. I developed a newfound respect for salespeople. And I remained in sales, mainly because I made so much money.

Having jumped into the pool, I lost some of my fear and loathing of sales a profession. Before taking the leap myself, I believed that most successful salespeople depended almost 100% on natural talent, good looks, a gift for gab, and a winning personality.

I had none of these traits.

After my preconceptions about sales and successful salespeople had effectively been demolished I quickly learned that salespeople tend to have strong opinions about what works and what doesn't work in sales. As a rule, salespeople do seem to have strong egos and strong opinions about just about everything. A strong ego is probably necessary for survival in the role, so it goes with the territory.

Opinions about what does and what doesn't work in sales seemed particularly strong though, even given the nature of the people who held them. Salespeople seemed to cling to their personal set of beliefs with particular intensity, almost like a drowning person might cling to a life preserver in heavy seas.

I couldn't help but be influenced by what I heard, and was pulled into the gravitational field of these powerful personalities. If they were successful, who was I to question their methods?

But occasionally two top salespeople would say exactly the opposite thing. It seemed to me they couldn't both be right. In my engineering mind, I wondered if the opposing points of view just proved that the particular variable under discussion wasn't really significant. In other words, it wouldn't really matter whether I followed Successful Salesperson #1's advice or Successful Salesperson #2's advice. It wouldn't materially affect the outcome.

I began to try to figure out which variables did in fact matter, and did in fact impact the outcomes of my sales endeavors.

In my early career as a salesperson I learned a little bit about direct mail and was introduced to the concept of a multi-variable experiment.

The basic concept looks like this:

	Mail Piece A	Mail Piece B
List A	1000 of piece A to list A Responses - 2	1000 of piece B to list A Responses - 6
List B	1000 of piece A to list B Responses - 3	1000 of piece B to list B Responses - 11

You would develop two different mail pieces, perhaps a postcard for "A" and a personal letter for "B" and mail to two different lists.

A quick inspection of the response rates in each quadrant shows that Mail Piece B in this example clearly worked best. And clearly List B, which had higher response rates in both cases, was the better list.

Marketing experts, like salespeople, tend to have strong opinions about what will work and what won't. For example, a lot of marketers emphasize fancy graphics and a slick, polished, professional piece. In my experimentation, I found that expensive, fancy pieces did not actually pull well. Simpler pieces pulled better. I also concluded that many marketers (understandably) emphasize the "creative" component that they enjoy. Both marketers and salespeople can benefit from experimentation.

If you start thinking about it, there are dozens of variables you can test. And if you do test them, sometimes you find results that are counter to what "the experts" say. When you drag opinions or expectations into the world of facts through research, you may be surprised by the results. But facts are facts. They are undeniable. And they are extremely useful if you are focused on results rather than on validating an opinion you hold dear.

Over the three years I experimented with direct mail, I was able to triple my response rate from 2% to 6%. While that, by itself, may not seem exciting, it was the front-end lead generation engine that fed my business. Leads for my business were the scarcest commodity. Tripling the leads tripled the contacts I made, the sales calls I made, and my top line. As with most businesses, tripling my top line more than tripled margins and my personal income.

But even this good news isn't the real point of my story. One day I asked myself, "What if I apply this same rigor to the sales process?" It was easy to translate the direct mail methods to cold calling. The only difference from my previous diagram was to change Piece A or B to Call Approach A or B.

As I began to experiment with calling approaches, I made some interesting discoveries. I found that the old "steam roller" approach ("Don't ever give them a chance to hang up!") wasn't as effective as playfully saying right up front, "My name is Steve. This is a sales call. Would you like to hang up?" Some people were put off by the approach. Some hung up. About 70%, though, chuckled a little and let me proceed, with permission.

In the end I concluded that the strong opinions of top salespeople, as dearly as they cling to them, were pretty much meaningless except as the possible basis for experimentation. And as my experiments proceeded, I found that what really works in selling is:

1. not what you are often told by salespeople or "experts,"
2. hard to discover, and
3. often the opposite of our natural tendencies, and always requires a reprogramming of our natural response patterns.

If you rebel at the idea of selling or being seen as a salesperson (like I did), you will tend to avoid it. That means your practice will languish through periods of feast and famine as you move through the inevitable cycles of doing the work when you have it, and scrambling to find new work when you don't.

At some point you may try to solve the problem by hiring a salesperson. While the salesperson may work out, typically they don't. And you still end up doing most of the sales. An Emory University study in which I participated indicated that technical organizations that succeed tend to have a senior principal who is sales focused, considers himself or herself a "seller," and often has a sales (non-technical) background. Like it or not, you're probably going to have to sell.

My experimentation continues today. I don't think I have all of the answers. I also don't think the target is static. I'm alive to the possibility that what works today may not be the best solution two years from now. However, the fact that you are reading this book suggests you may want some new insights right now. I think you'll be able to draw from my experience in two ways.

First, toss out your strongly-held opinions and begin experimenting. Take whatever you do now, dream up some alternatives, and test them. As a bit of practical advice, look at your sales process and figure out where the current bottlenecks are. Perhaps, like so many firms, you have a bottleneck at the beginning of the process: Leads. You just need someone who's willing to sit down and talk to you.

It may be later in the process: Separating tire kickers from buyers, for example. Or perhaps deciding which opportunities to pursue and which ones not to. Or what salespeople call "closing," or getting commitments in return for the effort you've invested in sales calls, referrals, proposals, and free consulting. Pick the spot and try something new.

Also, realize that symptoms often masquerade as causes. It's not always where you fall down that matters. Sometimes it's where you slipped earlier in the process that led to the fall. Where you see a failure point, you may need to try testing options at some point upstream in the process, prior to the actual problem. You don't lose a sale at the end of the cycle. That's just when you find out.

Second, I will share with you the results of my experimentation over the last 25 years. Since I have spent the last 20 years as a sales trainer, I have the advantage of having had the chance to move beyond personal experimentation to organizational level research.

This has allowed me to test and prove not only that a concept is valid, but also that it can be reproduced successfully across an organization.

INTRODUCTION

The CEO's point of view

I was asked to speak at an event for young CEOs. As we were mingling, I heard one young CEO say, "I have been through so many salespeople! None of them work out."

Another said, "Yeah! I just fired one. He had produced no business in six months. I think I was funding a professional tri-athlete!"

A third said, "I've had ten salespeople and just fired the tenth!"

The tone of the conversation was: "What is wrong with salespeople?"

These young CEOs did not seem to question their own role. They did not ask, "What is wrong with me?"

The assumption is that if it's not working it's the sales team's fault.

The CEO makes fundamental decisions that impact sales more than anything the sales department can do.

Steve Kraner

A typical startup sales model

1. Hire some salespeople
2. Set them loose on the market
3. Fire them for non-performance
4. Repeat as necessary

A team sport

In 1979, Bill Walsh was hired as head coach of the San Francisco 49ers. The 49ers had posted a dreadful 2-14 record the previous year, and did the same again in Walsh's first year. The difference between these two seasons, except for the record, was by all accounts vast. Walsh brought a system, and with it hope. By 1989, when Walsh left them, the San Francisco 49ers had won three Super Bowls. He and his team had become bona fide legends. He did it by forging a team.

With a football team, a system is essential. Process matters. Planning matters. Practice matters. Leaving outcomes to fate (or worse, luck) is risky at best. Relying on superstars to win the day is usually unreliable, and almost always unsustainable. Teams are built, bit by indispensable bit. That's what Bill Walsh did with the 49ers.

The same holds true, perhaps more so, in sales. And in fact, for your business as a whole. Building a successful corporate sales structure, or system, is not unlike building a successful sports team. The truth of the matter is that once a business grows beyond the lone capacity of the successful entrepreneur, selling becomes a team sport.

Flying by the seat of your pants precedes crashing by the seat of your pants.
— Bill Walsh, coach of the San Francisco 49ers

It starts with the CEO

I recently visited two clients. Both of them lead entrepreneurial companies. Company A built a sales team, got rid of them, did it again, and got rid of them again. Company B built a company with a sales team, sold it, and they are now building a second company.

8

One of the obvious differences between the two is that Company A was founded by a CEO with an operations background. Company B was founded by a CEO with a sales background. CEO A does not like sales and tries to hire other people to do it for him. CEO B likes selling, is actively involved in the sales process, teaches, coaches, and manages his sales team, and consistently produces salespeople who succeed.

Again, as the aforementioned study done by Emory University concluded, organizations led by technology- or product-focused leaders tend to fail, while those led by sales-focused leaders tend to succeed.

It's my observation that many tech companies are started by people with a technology bent and many (like me in 1989) don't like the sales side of the business. It is common for the founder to resist mastering sales.

If the owner is sales-averse, he must overcome his natural resistance to selling. Or else fail. Founders have to do a lot that's not their preference, or even in their basic nature.

On the other hand, if the founder is a great natural salesperson, he often finds he has trouble growing because he's limited to his own ability to sell, and is unable to replicate his success.

In either case, companies don't grow in smooth upward lines. They grow in a series of steps, and each step involves climbing a sheer cliff. The first step on the journey from owner-operator to walk-away business requires a sales process.

A process enables the natural salesperson to replicate his success, which in turn enables the uninitiated to succeed. A process enables training and coaching. A process allows the CEO to monitor, measure, and improve results.

Where the leadership is sales-averse

I worked at DEC when Ken Olsen was the CEO. He is reputed

to have said, "Salespeople are a necessary evil." With that sort of outlook, he created a company in which salespeople were looked down upon. The good salespeople tended to leave. When DEC lost its temporary technical advantage it quickly failed. In the late '80s and early '90s, if your resume said DEC most sales organizations wouldn't hire you. If it said Oracle, you were a hot commodity.

I see companies run by sales-averse leaders every day. The sales department is relegated to a dusty corner. The function is often pushed on the newest people. In some cases, sales is run by a salesperson who is doing more harm than good, but the CEO hates sales so much he won't get involved. The company is held hostage by Tommy Boy. (Rent the movie and you'll understand.)

Why hiring is not the solution

A CEO said to me, "I don't like to sell and I don't have to sell. I'll hire the right person and give them the right incentive. It will work."

Will it?

Successful salespeople are somewhere being successful. What is the right incentive that would convince a successful person to leave their pipeline of business and stream of commissions to work for your no-name, statistically-likely-to-fail startup?

The CEO, by contrast, has a powerful incentive: To build his company.

No one is going to do the tough work required for your company's success but you.

Avoiding selling

Those who don't like to sell avoid selling. Attempts to avoid selling include:

- Outsourcing sales

- Selling through channels (too soon)
- Hiring salespeople and setting them loose on the market
- Spending tons of money on marketing

You have to be the first salesperson

The first successful salesperson is typically one of the founders. My experience is that if you can't sell it you can't teach others to sell it. You can't build a sales team that works. You can't effectively manage an outsourced sales effort. Once you've blazed the path, you can define and document the sales process.

If you rely on someone else to provide a process as critical as sales, then the most common result is failure.

1 DEVELOPING YOUR SALES TEAM

Your Sales Team

Selling system

The selling system is the basis for your sales team. Everything else—the sales force structure, picking the people, training, coaching, and managing—all sit on top of (and come after) the system.

Once the system is in order, the next steps can be taken. All else follows.

As you can see in the illustration, the selling system is the foundation block of a six-level hierarchical model of the sales function on which you will build your sales team. Please understand that I do not use the term hierarchical lightly. I've patterned your sales team step pyramid after the idea behind Maslow's hierarchy of needs in the psychology of human motivation. In essence, the requirements lower down in the hierarchy must be met before the ones higher up can be attended to properly.

When summing up the legacy of legendary 49ers coach Bill Walsh, Scott Pioli (assistant general manager of the Atlanta Falcons) had this to say: "Build a system that would outlast the leaders, build something great. It wasn't just the one leader; build a system so great, the winning continued after he left … there was this idea to build something that will last while you're there and last beyond you."

Strategic marketing

Before we go any further, I need to point out that the sales team superstructure (including the selling system), along with the rest of the company, sits on top of a wider corporate foundation: Strategic marketing.

I've found as I work with clients that if they haven't handled strategic marketing correctly then the sales team may never get off the ground. While marketing is not technically part of the sales team pyramid, it is the main supplier of all that is necessary to keep the team on (or in) the field and in the game.

After we take a careful look at each step of the sales hierarchy, we will take some time to consider the importance of strategic marketing, and ensuring that the sales and marketing functions are operating smoothly in mutually supportive and beneficial ways.

Sales force structure

On a football field, you'll need an offense (including a quarterback, running backs, wide receivers, linemen, and so on), a defense (linemen, ends, cornerbacks, a safety, et. al.), and special teams (kick returner, punt returner, long snapper, etc.) Each position requires a particular set of physical, mental, and psychological attributes, and each requires a particular set of core skills. Many of the skills are transferrable, but not all of them.

The same is true (albeit to a much lesser extent—but it's the same in principle) of the sales team. The sales structure is determined by a process in the same way that the objectives and rules of football define the players' positions with their roles and functions.

Salesperson is a broad term, a bit like "football player." The former may conjure images of an outgoing, fast-talking, glad-hander (I hope we are past that no longer true and rather unfair perception, but alas, I held that view myself). The latter likely evokes thoughts of a very large, very powerful, possibly ham-handed athlete. As with salespeople, the image is a parody and for the most part inaccurate.

The truth is that a quarterback is largely unlike a center or a field goal kicker. You probably wouldn't hire a really fast and agile runner to kick field goals, or a gigantic hard-hitting tackler to throw touchdown passes. There are likewise a lot of "sales" jobs and they require different attributes and behaviors to succeed.

One excellent salesperson may be able to master many or even most of the skillsets required for a broad spectrum of sales functions, but the importance of delineating each specific role and the specific successful behaviors associated with it cannot be overemphasized.

People

Once the sales force structure is determined, and each role is well defined, you can pick the right people. The following excerpt from my coaching journal illustrates the connection between the system and hiring the right people:

I was doing a mock hiring interview with the CEO of an IT staffing company when he stopped the interview and said: "I'm clearly failing the interview, and I know it. I just had an epiphany. It's easy to interview technical people. You ask them if they know something, and they either know it or they don't. They can't fool you. The problem with salespeople is that there is no clear right or wrong. There is no way to ask a question to which there is a clear-cut answer. You ask general questions and they give vague answers. If it feels warm and fuzzy, you hire them."

He went on to say, *"If you see sales as a science and not black magic, and if you use a sales process or system, then you can conduct a sales interview in the same way you conduct a technical interview. You can ask specific questions and determine if they know or they don't. With a system for selling in place, I can hire salespeople as well as I do technical people."*

The Right People Matter

"The old adage 'People are your most important asset' is wrong. The right people are you're your most important asset."

— Jim Collins, *Turning Goals into Results*

Training

Once you have the right person in a clearly-defined role you can train them on the best way to perform the role.

Here's a typical three step sales training at a startup:

1. Here's your desk
2. Here's your phone
3. Good luck!

Another example from my coaching notebook makes the point:

An entrepreneur said, "I only have one rep on my team who is worth a darn."

I asked what behavior separated that rep from the others and he said, "That's easy. He picks up the phone and gets appointments."

I asked what process he taught his salespeople to make the outbound calls.

He said, "I don't. That's Sales 101. I hire for that."

Obviously this CEO had no idea how to make the outbound calls himself. He was like a basketball coach shouting, "Get tall!"

Management with no system results in lots of pressure, but no help. Such a manager adds no value.

Coaching

Teaching delivers knowledge. Training applies knowledge to skills, and provides a safe space to practice new skills and get professional feedback. Coaching ensures mastery of a skill.

Another entry from my sales coaching notebook reminds me of what an entrepreneurial CEO said about himself after sitting through a sales training program:

"Before this program, when my people asked for help with sales I would say things like, 'Have you tried coming in on a Saturday?'"

He went on to say, "With a selling system in place, a common process, and a common language, now I can help them. I can ask if they followed the process. I can observe calls or debrief calls and find the failure points. Further, now it's about the process and not the person, so I can coach them without harming their self-esteem."

Many early stage CEOs who also act as the sales manager add no value, because they don't know how.

Most salespeople avoid accountability because coaching has for them always come in the form of pressure, not help.

Managing

Like a good head coach keeps tweaking and improving the team playbook, you should continuously inspect your sales process. A system allows you to pick leading indicators which will sustain an effective management dashboard for your sales process.

While managing and coaching may seem like redundant terms, there is a point at which your most senior salespeople may not need much coaching, but you have to keep some degree of management in place forever.

Coaching ensures mastery of a skill in the learning phase. Managing ensures continuous application of the system by everyone.

Conclusion

As the CEO, whether you are a superb salesperson or you hate selling, you have not optimized the sales function until you have a defined and documented selling system in place. Once you have a selling system, everything else sits on that foundation.

Building a company is about building systems in every functional area, including sales.

2 WITHOUT A SELLING SYSTEM

When your current sales team asks for more marketing, beware. They may or may not know what is needed. They may ask for:

- More marketing
- Better literature
- Lower prices
- New features
- More pre-sales tech support

These things are crutches. If they don't know how to sell, you can never give them enough crutches. You will spend a lot of money and time doing things that don't address the core weakness.

What's limiting your sales

When I ask what currently constrains sales, salespeople generally say:

- Lack of time
- Insufficient leads
- Competition that is better or cheaper
- Too few sales engineers or other resources
- The fact that the new version isn't ready

- The prices are too high
- The economy is weak

They never say, "It's because I am not skilled at using a sales process."

An agitated mongoose in your lap

I was supervising live outbound calls at a medium-sized software company. The top sales rep did what I asked him to do and after a couple of dials he got a potential buyer on the phone. The buyer began to describe a problem the rep's software could solve. When the buyer started to open up, the sales rep reacted as if an agitated mongoose had just landed in his lap. He immediately ended the call by offering to send literature.

Unfortunately, this was not at all unusual. I observe live calls and listen to call recordings frequently. The salesperson who "bails out" is more typical than a salesperson who can sustain a dialogue that will lead to a sale. Salespeople bail out before buyers do.

Consider this constraint: sales skill

This particular salesperson I was observing had gotten to be the top rep by virtue of being a hard worker. He made a lot of calls, got put off, sent literature, followed up (pestered), and hoped. He also took inbound calls, inflicted a standard pitch on everyone, and then required them to endure a standard demo. After this, some would still buy.

He was digging a hole with a bowling ball and he was very comfortable and committed to it.

Let's take a look at some of the commonly perceived limiting factors in a sales environment as compared to the genuine constraints that remain hidden or are glossed over by the misconceptions or otherwise ill-conceived explanations and excuses.

Perceived Constraint	Real Constraint
Insufficient leads	Salespeople cannot talk about the customer's world. The buyer has to mentally translate how the seller's laundry list of solutions applies to their world. Most buyers will not make this effort. Leads are not converted at the rate they should be.
S.E.'s or pre-sales support staff	Salespeople use resources on losing deals because they cannot differentiate opportunities from lost causes.
Literature	Salespeople cannot sustain a two-way dialogue with their customers, so they depend on literature to sell for them.
Time	Reps are unnecessarily extending the sales cycle by terminating effective conversations in favor of sending literature, premature presentations and demonstrations, and writing proposals.
Price	When selling becomes presenting, all solutions look the same and price becomes the only differentiator.
Competition	The competition's salesperson out sold your salesperson.
The economy	If your salespeople are dependent on inbound calls, and that stream slows down, sales will fall. If they are weak at building value in a good economy, they'll fail when it's tougher.

Perceived Constraint	Real Constraint
New version is late	In a selling model where selling = pitching, the reps want to pitch the latest and greatest, hoping new features will make selling easier. As soon as they learn anything about the new version, they focus on it, tell customers about it, and then *can't close anything based on your current capabilities.*

Sales creativity

In the mind of the struggling salesperson, factors out of their control constrain sales. But these are really just symptoms. Salespeople use their creative capacity, as we all do, to avoid admitting to shortcomings. Our egos support false beliefs.

And customers feed them excuses they can repeat. Just like a game show host, they give the losing reps a "lovely parting gift" such as:

- "You had the best technical fit, and you lost because of internal politics. The boss has a relationship with your competition."
- "I would have picked you, but your competition came in so much lower that purchasing made us go with them."
- "The economy is just so bad, we can't do it!"

You cannot be swayed by these destructive freebies (masquerading as kind sentiments) from would-be customers. You must address the real problem.

The core weakness is lack of a defined and repeatable selling system and people who are good at executing the process.

Note to entrepreneurs who enjoy selling: If you are a natural salesperson, your success cannot be replicated unless it is reduced to a process.

3 THE SELLING SYSTEM: BIG PICTURE

Why is selling difficult?

"It is easier to train for content than collaboration."
— *David Nadler, Chairman of Delta Consulting*

One of the features of being human you may have noticed is that you win all of the arguments in your head.

Selling is difficult because there is at least one other person involved. It requires more than knowledge; it requires mastery of skills. Almost everyone can learn to give a presentation. Few master collaboration. Even fewer master persuasion.

Ed Bradley of "60 Minutes" asked Tiger Woods why golf is so hard. Tiger said, "There are a lot of moving parts."

A sales cycle is like a golf swing. Closing a sale involves a lot of moving parts. And the bigger it is, the more parts there are. Some sales cycles are simple and short. Some are long and complex. They are all like an equation:

$$A \times B \times C \times D = Sale$$

If any variable is zero, then there is no sale. You can do a lot of things right and still lose. The more complex the sales cycle, the more variables, the greater the chance something is overlooked.

A consistently successful sales rep attended my Sales Bootcamp for the fourth time. He said, "It's taken me years to have this light bulb, but as I sit here today, I realize you can't just pick bits and pieces of this system and expect success. You have to use the whole system and all of the tactics."

He's right. One uncovered base, one zero in the equation, and the process fails.

A system makes sure you cover all the bases, like a pilot's pre-flight checklist. Surgical outcomes are being improved today through the use of checklists in the operating room. I recommend sales leaders read *The Checklist Manifesto*, by Atul Gawande. It is perhaps not a compelling title, but it is a compelling read. Behind great performance is great process.

The book begins with "The problem of extreme complexity." The more complex the process, the more the need for systems and checklists. As one of many examples, Gawande points out that the B-17 Flying Fortress was so complex it was initially considered to be unflyable. As if to prove the point, it crashed in an early demo. That mishap is the reason every cockpit has a book of checklists today.

Selling is also complex. Salespeople ought never make the mistake of considering themselves flyable by the seat of their pants. They ought instead to take steps to avoid crashing.

Tiger Woods didn't invent a new way to swing a golf club. He diligently learned the best way known and became a master of using a system to control all of the moving parts.

Since the time of the Greeks

"The leader must himself believe that willing obedience always beats forced obedience and that he can get this only by knowing what should be done.

Then he can secure obedience from his men because he can convince them he knows best." — Xenophon, Cyropaedia, *c. 360 BC*

The entrepreneur violates this rule when he:

- Tells his team to do things that he himself cannot do.
- Gives non-specific, vague advice, like "Get creative!" and "Smile and dial!"

Leaders recognize the importance of this rule when they:

- Have proven processes to replicate success.
- Can offer specific, actionable advice.
- Lead by example.

There is no X-factor

I sat next to a self-proclaimed CEO consultant on a flight from San Francisco once, and he was working as we flew. He had his papers all over the tray table and it was getting into my seat a bit, so he apologized. I noticed that he had pictures of CEOs, and one of the CEOs was someone I knew. We got to talking about his work.

He was researching the question, "Do CEOs make a difference?" I asked him whether he thought they do, and if so, why he thought so. He had decided that they do based on the fact that new CEOs often come in and turn a company around. Unfortunately, the opposite also occurred. He concluded that in his study of successful and unsuccessful CEOs, the difference was not vision, but execution; the mundane, day-to-day details of how to get it done.

My seatmate's name was Ram Charam. His work was published in the Harvard Business Review, and then in his book *Execution: The Discipline of Getting Things Done.*

There is no "X-factor." It's about process and systems and discipline.

The origin of selling systems

John Henry Patterson, the founder of National Cash Register (now NCR Corporation), is regarded as the father of modern selling. He had a retail shop with no point-of-sale cash control. He bought a cash register to mitigate that deficiency, and quickly realized the machine's value. So he bought the rights to the cash register, founded NCR, and successfully sold cash registers. He then hired salespeople and found that they failed.

Many entrepreneurs stop at just that point, after one or multiple attempts to move beyond dependence on the owner as the chief salesperson. Rather than quit or stay small, Patterson decided to seek help.

Based on a handbook written by his brother-in-law, Patterson established the world's first sales training school on the grounds of the NCR factory campus at Sugar Camp in Dayton, Ohio. This is the first known written selling system.

Patterson's innovation—the selling system—propagated from NCR to IBM, and to Xerox, and beyond as his employees left to start their own ventures. Walter A. Friedman's, *Birth of a Salesman: The Transformation of Selling in America*, provides a comprehensive and enjoyable telling of the history of selling.

Today, you don't necessarily need to work as hard as Patterson did. Or at least you don't have to start from scratch like he did. The science of selling has advanced dramatically. Selling systems have been perfected and are available for sale. You don't have to reinvent the wheel, as they say. You just have to find what's out there and tailor it to your company and market. The process is as knowable as a zone defense or a recipe to make pancakes.

The evolution of selling systems

The first selling systems used the following basic process:

1. Present

2. Handle the inevitable stalls and objections
3. Close

In the 1960s, almost a century after Patterson invented the selling system, a wave of new thinking arose. One of the thought leaders was a behavioral psychologist named Neil Rackham. Unlike other authors of sales books, most of whom were salespeople, Rackham was a scientist who spent 12 years observing and documenting what salespeople actually do. He described some of his findings in *SPIN Selling*, one of the great sales books of all time.

Thinkers of that era decided that it was better to start with an understanding of the customer, so they proposed a system that looked like this:

1. Qualify
2. Present
3. Close

Comparing the early selling systems to traditional consultative selling systems

	Early Selling Systems	Traditional Consultative Selling Systems
1	Present	Qualify
2	Handle stalls and objections	Present
3	Close	Close

There are two major reasons traditional consultative selling systems proved more effective than the original.

First, the salesperson recovered lost time that was otherwise squandered on buyers who were not qualified.

Second, the presentation in the updated system is informed by information the seller has gained from the buyer. It is a more targeted presentation, based on facts provided by the buyer.

Notice the traditional consultative approach has no step for handling stalls and objections. Most stalls and objections are the result of premature presentations. People don't argue with their own data.

Always be closing

I am calling them "Traditional Consultative Selling Systems" because they are not state-of-the art. Almost all of them required a "close" at the end, and the close involved some sort of pressure or manipulation. Only Neil Rackham stood adamantly against closing techniques of any kind, and he was initially ridiculed for it.

In the 1960s, '70s, and '80s, "closing" was widely considered a technique. A sales move. And the various closes had names:

- The Assumptive Close
- The Alternative Event Close
- The Ben Franklin Close
- The Puppy Dog Close

Sales experts at that time taught phrases and gimmicks designed to get prospects to say yes. The problem of course is that in complex sales these closing methods often backfired because buyers felt manipulated and pressured.

Because most people avoid conflict, buyers under pressure may agree to a purchase; they may allow themselves to be shoe-horned into agreeing to something. But they won't be happy about it. And that does not make for a good, long-term relationship. In fact, it undermines any future sales with that buyer.

And what's more, today's buyer won't put up with that sort of bullying behavior. If you try these tactics today you may leave thinking you did a good job, but they won't let you back in the door. If your sales cycle is more than one call, you'll lose.

As a side note, I think it's important to mention that Patterson's system was quite likely the most sensible approach in his day and age. If I must carry around my cash registers on a mule cart, and travel ten dusty miles from Chillicothe to Frankfurt, it seems entirely reasonable that I'd want to "qualify in" rather than "qualify out." It may well be the best use of my time. And in face-to-face selling with a one-call sales cycle, pressure tactics do in fact work.

In a world of phones and cars (and airplanes), however, being selective makes a whole lot more sense, and is a far better use of time and effort. And in an extended sales cycle, pressure tactics will ensure only that you'll never get back in for a second call.

Patterson was a man of his time, and a man ahead of his time. It's hard to argue with success.

State-of the-art

Closing is not part of a modern selling system. Modern buyers are not going to respond well to Alternative Event closes, Puppy Dog closes, Impending Event closes, etc. The days of Alec Baldwin's famous "always be closing" rant in the movie *Glengarry Glen Ross* are long gone.

Language is important, and the term "closing" drives the wrong thoughts and behaviors. Today, top salespeople co-build a mutual action plan with buyers, a plan that both parties agree to and work together to reach a well-considered conclusion.

State-of-the-art selling systems look like this:

1. Qualify
2. Co-build a mutual action plan
3. Deliver proof as determined in the mutual action plan

This process is in the best interest of both the seller and the buyer. Building the bridge from analysis to action *is* the close.

The Buyer's Journey

The best way to generate new leads that are easy to close is by taking care of your current customers. A state-of-the art selling system understands the buyer's journey.

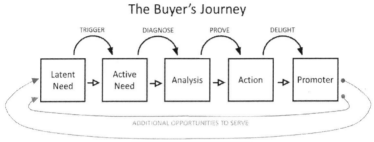

The Buyer's Journey

Three Sales Bridges

Buyers can (and often do) progress through all five stages of the sales journey on their way to a purchase—and to becoming a promoter—without any help at all. But the chances of them negotiating the gaps smoothly, without any assistance, are relatively low. With a skilled sales guide alongside to help them bridge the gaps, buyers are far more likely to have easier, quicker, and more successful purchasing experiences. Ideally, the gaps can be successfully crossed with three bridging conversations.

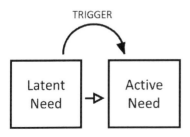

The trigger conversation

The first job of a salesperson who has uncovered a new selling opportunity (whether in "hunter" mode dealing with an unknown prospect, or as a "trusted adviser" dealing with a long-term client) is to be the trigger that causes a buyer to discover the urgency of a particular latent need, and spur in them a strong desire to take action.

Note this carefully because it is very key: People do not buy because something sounds good or interesting or even beneficial; people buy when they become personally emotionally invested in the change that an investment or purchase promises to produce. Intellectual arguments will not win a sale; people buy on emotion.

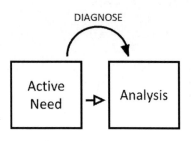

The diagnostic conversation

Once a buyer is primed and ready to make a change, the wise seller will slow the process down. The bridge between the buyer's recognition of an active need and her own analysis of the solution set is the seller's assistance with a thorough diagnosis of the need. This is where mistakes are most often made, and where the seller really earns his money. It is also the place where buyers most often fall into a ditch. Diagnosing often goes wrong for two main reasons:

1. Buyers don't think deeply enough about the problem or opportunity (and thus tend to default to a knee-jerk reaction).

2. Buyers (like nearly everybody else) don't like vulnerability and therefore are not always forthcoming or entirely honest with sellers or even themselves.

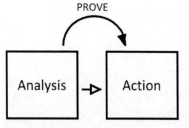

The proof conversation: Co-building a mutual action plan)

The next great challenge on the buyer's journey is the move from analysis to action. It's a huge chasm. The only bridge that will reliably span it is proof. Otherwise it will require an Evel Knievel leap, which while perhaps exciting is notoriously unreliable. The best proof available is a mutual action plan (MAP), the product of a cooperative effort between buyer and seller. It's no good telling a buyer that some data point or some factual information is proof; people believe what they want to believe.

We shall consider these three sales bridges in detail in Chapter 5, Selling System Essentials, Part 1: The Tactical Selling Playbook.

Comparing strategic and tactical selling systems

Tactical selling is about doing things right.

Strategic selling means doing the right things, with the right people, at the right time.

You can be tactically brilliant and still make a strategic blunder. A common example is to give a superb presentation to the wrong person who then denies access to the key people, while your competition seizes the high ground and wins.

Tactical selling

Tactical selling is what you do when you are with a customer. Tactical selling systems are about *execution* and are represented by the arrow labeled Execute in the figure.

Tactical selling is about doing things right; it's about action; it's about execution.

Every company with direct salespeople needs a tactical sales process. High velocity sales environments require a tactical system only.

A tactical selling system provides structure for the three sales conversations that bridge the gaps in the buyer's journey: the trigger conversation, the diagnostic conversation, and co-building a mutual action plan (the proof conversation). The bridge over the fourth gap, from Action to Promoter, may be part of the sales role, but is usually assigned to customer success managers. A prescribed process for delighting the customer and ensuring that buyers become promoters is vital to the overall tactical system.

It is well to remember here that tactical selling is largely counterintuitive. In sales, our nature often works against us. Why? Because selling is opposite of our nature. We have both good and bad instincts. If a foreign object approaches our eyes, we blink without thinking. That unthinking reaction protects us. It's a good thing.

But in a car crash, our natural reaction is to brace for impact. Ironically, a drunk person is more likely to survive a car crash without injury precisely because his reactions are slowed. When paratroopers go to Fort Benning, the first thing they have to learn is how to fall correctly. Our natural reaction is wrong and will result in injury. Selling is likewise largely counterintuitive.

We all need a process that trains us to do what works rather than what we think or feel ought to work.

Find a tactical selling system, master it, and make it part of your company culture.

Some tactical selling systems for consideration include those described in books such as:

- *SPIN Selling* by Neil Rackham
- *Solution Selling* by Michael Bosworth
- *The Challenger Sale* by Brent Adamson and Matthew Dixon

You can also create a custom sales process, powered by the High-Tech Selling System I offer. This process is tuned for software and SAS companies because it is tuned to selling technology to the enterprise. The public version of this program is offered in my Software Sales Bootcamp (www.softwaresalesgurus.com).

Strategic selling

Great salespeople have a bias for action. I'd like to count myself in that group. But we can't take a "fire, ready, aim" approach to pursuing the larger opportunities.

Strategic selling, as I said, means doing the right things, with the right people, at the right time. It's about what you do when you are NOT with a customer. It means you must plan what you are going to do (how you are going to execute), and it means you must regularly review what you are doing and how things are working out.

A strategic selling system provides the tools to help you *plan* and *review.*

Plan: Strategic selling systems require planning prior to action. Planning ensures we get ready first, then aim, then fire. Strategic programs ask us to take pains to understand the customer, their organization, their politics, and their business. Planning includes understanding who the critical path players in the decision process are, what their preferences are, how best to approach them, and how to build consensus in a complex selling environment.

Review: Since no plan survives first contact with reality, a review process after every action is required to adjust the plan. Athletes watch game film. Military leaders are taught to do after-action assessments. Salespeople need to do the same.

Sales reviews:

- Provide a dispassionate assessment of the plan versus reality
- Reveal problems and new information
- Feed into the next planning cycle

- Accelerate the learning curve of the sellers

Strategic selling systems are processes for planning and review. Some options for consideration include:

- *Strategic Selling* by Robert Miller and Stephen Heiman
- The "Target Account Selling" program by Target Marketing Systems (no book has been published)
- *Flawless Execution* by James D. Murphy

For years I referred people to these programs and they referred people to me. They are superb programs. However, experience indicates that the problem with strategic programs is that they are built for everyone, so they end up with a research and data entry load so large that no one has time to execute the program. Six months after the program launch, no one is filling out the planning sheets.

My solution to excessive research and data entry is to customize the program. Make it as light as possible by reducing the process to the minimum essentials. Then enforce its adoption through an ongoing mastery phase. Your team will not embrace the process until they experience its value. Success is the ultimate motivator in sales.

Three things to think about before implementing a strategic selling system

A common complaint I hear is, "I trained my people in Miller-Heiman and six months later no one was doing the blue sheets and gold sheets!"

There are three reasons for this, and it's not a programmatic flaw:

1. **Strategy first.** If you train the strategic before you have tactical basics in place, you will fail. It's like a football team with a great play book, but no blocking and tackling. If you assume that tactical selling is Sales 101, and your folks already have it, you are always wrong. NFL coaches are working on the basics every training camp, and going back

to them when they review every game film.

2. **One and done never works.** You have to make the process part of the culture and that starts with you, then your managers, and then your salespeople. A two-day training process will not drive change. You need a one-year process that starts with buy-in at the management level, attains buy-in at the sales level, then supports and reinforces the process to drive change.

3. **No manager training.** When Cesar Millan, the Dog Whisperer, fixes a dog behavior problem, he always starts with the owner. If you want your salespeople to do the right thing, make sure you start with the managers.

How to master a selling system

Learning to sell is like learning to golf or play the guitar. It requires knowledge and mastery of skills. It takes time and the learning curve is painful. If you've ever played soccer, you know it takes years to really master the skills.

Here's how you master a selling system, in a nutshell:

1. Read the book.
2. Attend a training session.
3. Use the skills and concepts in your day-to-day selling.
4. Customize the process to your world.
5. Document the final process.

Where the selling system fits in your company

The sales process is part of a larger corporate system that includes (but is not limited to) developing products and/or services, marketing, selling, and delivering those products and/or services, all undergirded by strategic marketing. A company that has not streamlined its processes will tend to see unnecessary (and often counterproductive) overlap, usually between its marketing, sales, and customer service efforts.

The marketing function may inadvertently get involved in selling through, for example, uncoordinated direct mail campaigns. Sellers may feel compelled (or forced) to generate leads for themselves, or to try to control the delivery process.

It is important to define each process and carefully delineate the specific roles, functions, and activities that fall under its purview. This will ensure that there are no gaps between them, and that each process feeds the next in proper sequence. It's best if everyone works from one central set of customer information.

Another reason to deliberately outline each process at this level is to identify and eliminate redundant or conflicting efforts.

The marketing and sales interface

Marketing, ideally, will view sales as its customer in the areas where marketing feeds into the sales process. Sales and marketing need to work closely to define and agree on what constitutes a lead.

Areas of joint sales and marketing concern are:

- The customer database
- Lists
- Lead generation
- Lead nurturing

- Sales training
- Sales tools and collateral

The sales and delivery interface

A selling system should not stop with the purchase order. The delivery of the solution needs to resolve the customer's dissatisfaction. Their problem must be solved, their fear resolved, or their goal attained. The more demonstrable the impact, the easier future selling will be. Super-satisfied clients will produce a bumper crop of future business and referrals.

Resources

Before you design your selling system, you need to make fundamental decisions about your company. These decisions are in the realm of strategic marketing. The two classic books on this topic are:

1. *Crossing the Chasm* by Geoffrey Moore.
2. *The Discipline of Market Leaders* by Michael Treacy and Fred Wiersema.

For solid marketing help I recommend:

- The Chasm Group
- Pragmatic Marketing
- Evolve Marketing

4 CHOOSING AND CUSTOMIZING A SELLING SYSTEM

Your Sales Team

Even today many senior leaders insist sales is more art than science, so their sales efforts are powered by hunches and vague philosophies, not facts. The endless stream of sales fads come and go like bell bottoms, mullets and powdered wigs.

Effective selling is not primarily an art. It is primarily a science. Like good science, there is plenty of room for artistry, but our current understanding of neuroreceptors explains much of the physiology of influence and choice. We'll look at this a little more carefully in Chapter 5.

The selling system basics described in this chapter are rooted in split testing, third-party observation and brain science – the modern science of selling.

This chapter and the next provide a DYI guide for creating your own selling system. For those who prefer to do it that way, this is like a recipe in a cookbook. I will also selfishly point out that I offer these services and would be glad to guide you through the process.

Impact of the wrong versus right selling system

A CEO came up to me after I finished a talk. He told me that he and some associates had started a tech company and it had gone very well. The eldest of them acted as the sales VP and decided to retire. It was a graceful departure and they had plenty of time to find his successor. He said they were very picky and finally chose a new sales VP who had been successful in two prior tech companies. Within a year of his arrival, sales were down, most of the sales team had left, and the sales VP resigned.

The CEO asked what else he could have done.

Before I finish this story, allow me to propose a model. In the figure below is a range of selling environments. On one end of the matrix (to the left) is high velocity, simple sales. It's mostly about the transaction, and involves very little personal interaction with the customer. Too much process here would be like cutting butter with a chainsaw. A great example of too much process is excessive time spent on account and territory plans and hours researching potential clients.

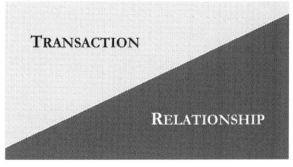

TRANSACTION	
	RELATIONSHIP

HIGH VELOCITY   HIGH INTIMACY

On the other extreme (the right side of the matrix) is the high intimacy sales cycle. It takes a lot of focus and effort to get a deal. It requires a high degree of customer insight and political alignment. Large deals require multiple decision-makers, executive involvement, long sales cycles, and formal purchasing processes. On this side of the matrix you are cutting down an oak, and you certainly don't want to use a butter knife. Here you should invest time planning and researching. We all operate somewhere within this matrix.

Back to the story. As we explored the CEO's plight, it became clear to me that the new sales VP had come from a high velocity, transactional selling environment. In his new role, he continued to do the things that made him successful in his old role—as we all do. In a more complex selling environment, his prior approach led to failure.

Velocity versus intimacy isn't the only significant variable in sales environments. Hunting (demand creation) versus inbound call handling (demand fulfillment) is another big differentiator.

DEMAND FULFILLMENT VS.	**DEMAND CREATION**

If you do as we consultants love to do—create a two-dimensional graph—you end up with:

Sales Environments

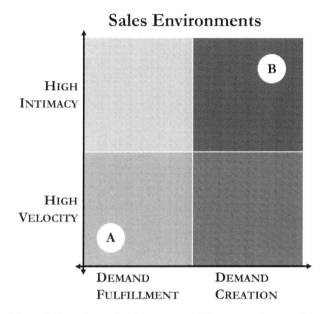

Now let's take a look at two different sales environments. Environment "A" in the diagram above might be an inbound call center at Dell. Dollar amounts of transactions are small and the products are relatively simple. If you have a reasonably non-offensive personality, you'll probably do well. You can use tactics like the assumptive close, "Will you be paying by credit card or purchase order?"

Environment "B" might be selling cloud-based ERP systems to the Fortune 500. These are complex, big dollar deals requiring senior levels of approval. These deals involve high risk to the buyer and they lean toward consensus decision-making to ensure proper due diligence and to spread the risk. In this environment, you must be a powerful person who can reach and influence senior people. Here tactics like high-pressure closing will ensure you get locked out after one meeting.

The system you choose will depend on the complexity of your sales cycle and the nature of demand creation.

Choosing and customizing your selling system

Once again, there is no reason at all to reinvent the wheel. It would take a lifetime to reinvent how to sell. Start with an existing sales process.

As you begin your research, keep in mind everyone with a direct sales force needs a tactical sales system. Not everyone needs a strategic sales system.

How to tell if you need a strategic selling system

In general, high intimacy sales environments require both a tactical and a strategic selling system. Your sales cycle is a high-intimacy environment if:

- Your price point is high
- Multiple decision makers are involved
    o due to high price point
    o because your solution crosses functional silos in customer organizations
    o if you are selling to government organizations
- Your solution is hard to understand
- Your offering is new to the market
- Your solution is novel
- Deployment risk is high
- Your solution requires significant cultural change
- Your offering is highly customized
- The sales cycle requires more than three sales calls

Pick the lowest cost sales model: self-service/inside sales/field sales

Sales can be accomplished through a range of sales models. Each has an associated cost. Generally, as the complexity of the sales cycle increases, more customer intimacy is required and the cost of the sales model increases. The CEO should pick the lowest cost model that will get the job done.

Self-service: For small transactional purchases a web site that allows the customer to research and even try the product or service is appropriate. This is a self-service model.

Telesales: If the price point is higher or the decision more complex, customers may need some assistance making a decision. In this case a telesales system should work well.

Field sales: Where sales cycles are long, dollar values high, and more than one decision maker is involved, forward deployed field salespeople may be both justified and required for competitive reasons.

Customizing the selling system

One size fits nobody. The fact that you don't have to reinvent the wheel is good, but that doesn't mean you don't have to tailor the system to your company. Gather your top sales thought leaders for a one or two-day sales process development workshop. And walk them through this suggested process:

Step 1: Ask each person to break the current sales process into the typical, major steps required.

Step 2: Compare results and discuss the steps as a group. Expect divergent opinions. Allow for discussion and work toward a consensus model.

Step 3: For each step, define the sales goal and a reasonable test for completion. Ensure each test for completion is customer-validated. Measure customer activity, not sales activity. The best way to ensure quality as well as quantity is to verify the completion of the step with the customer. For example, this means shifting away from measuring how many proposals the sales team produced to how many mutual action plans were agreed to by customers.

At the end of each step, it should be noted that there are two possible outcomes. The first is your stated goal. The second is a *"no."* It's important to remind the salesperson and the buyer that "no" is always okay.

Step 4: Develop tactics for each step. Specifics are important in this phase.

Like a golf stroke, it is the fine points that can make or break a sale. What is obvious or intuitive to one person can be an epiphany to others.

Step 5: Develop tools for each step. Tools or job aides may include a perfect

> ### Details Matter
>
> "I wondered why it is that a request stated in a certain way will be rejected, while the same request that asks for the same favor in a slightly different fashion will be successful."
>
> —Robert Cialdini, *Influence: The Psychology of Persuasion*

discovery call checklist, a planning template, a negotiation preparation work sheet, or anything that helps you hardwire the sales process into the nervous system of your company. The tools required are typically a function of the activities required at each step of your sales process. Keep it light!

Step 6: Inventory the knowledge and skills required for each step, and ensure you have a training plan to deliver the required knowledge and a coaching process to build the skills over time.

Step 7: State with clarity the ethical underpinning of your selling system, and introduce those principles to your salespeople along with the process and tactics. Your system derives its power from the thought you put into your sales process, but even more from the ethical underpinning on which it is based. The impact of sales tactics is driven by the intent behind them.

Once completed, you will have a documented sales process that your salespeople can follow for each sale and that your managers can use as a basis for training, coaching, and managing.

Ethical underpinning

In Step 7 above I mentioned the importance of an ethical underpinning. That is not by accident. It matters. Sales techniques that are used without an ethical underpinning will almost always fail because people recognize (and abhor) selfishness and insincerity.

The fact is that your entire selling system needs to be based on a firm ethical foundation or it will flounder. Here is my suggested ethical underpinning for your sales system:

- Everything we do is in both the best interest of the customer and our company, every step of the way.
- Our sales approach is built on a disarming level of honesty.
- We diagnose first, then prescribe as needed. Anything else is malpractice.

Sample sales process

Here's a more complete view of the Buyer's Journey, juxtaposed with a sample sales process. It shows what the outcome of your sales process development workshop might look like:

Customer Buying Stage	Sales Bridge Step	Goal	Test for Completion	Activities	Tools	Tactics
Latent Need	Plan	Map territor/account and develop a team sales action plan.	Approved territory/account plan.	Territor/account planning. Plan briefings to peers and management.	Planning Templates: • Territor • Account • Opportunity	Involve everyone who touches the customer.
Active Need (Dissatisfaction)	Trigger Conversation (a.k.a. Prospecting)	Develop sufficient dissatisfaction to schedule a meeting.	An email to the customer recapping the conversation.	Research. Direct Mail. Phone Calls. Networking. Executive Events.	Seven-step outbound call process.	Tactics to: • Establish rapport • Take charge of the call • Uncover dissatisfaction
Analysis	Diagnostic Conversation (a.k.a. Qualification)	Mutual agreement on: • Need • Solution • Investment • Decision process.	An email to the customer recapping all of the key agreements.	Sales calls. Executive calls.	Perfect discovery call checklist. Mutual outcome plan template.	Tactics to: • Establish rapport • Take charge of the call • Uncover dissatisfaction • Discuss money • Co-build a mutual action plan (MAP)
Action	Co-build a Mutual Action Plan (a.k.a. Close)	Final agreement	Approved order	Co-execute the MAP. Demo's, Proposals, Presentations, etc.	Presentation templates. Proposal templates.	Tactics to deal with objections and concerns. A negotiation process, if needed.
Promoter	Delight (a.k.a. Service)	Super-satisfied client.	Reference account.	Co-create customer success plan.	Proactive account development planning template.	Anticipate and deal with transitional problems. Monitor for new needs.

The system is not linear

Note that the end of the process is service, with a goal of super-satisfying the client. If this goal is achieved, the super-satisfied client will have future needs and you will be well-positioned to serve them. The super-satisfied client is also a good source of referrals. So the end of the system feeds the front of the system with the highest quality leads.

5 SELLING SYSTEM ESSENTIALS, PART 1
THE TACTICAL SALES PLAYBOOK

As with any team sport, one of the differentiating factors between the championship team and all the other really excellent teams in the league is adherence to a truly stunning playbook. Playbooks are a weighty matter. A truly great playbook, flawlessly executed, will inspire both shock and awe; it cannot be ignored.

If you haven't seen Adam Sandler in *The Waterboy*, there's a wonderfully amusing (if mildly disturbing) scene that puts a fine point on the critical importance of the playbook. Coach Klein (Henry Winkler) of the South Central Louisiana State University Mud Dogs confesses the cause of all his failure as a coach, and in life, to Bobby Boucher (Sandler): 20 years earlier his archrival Red Beaulieu (Jerry Reed) had stolen his green notebook full of foolproof plays.

> Boucher: *"That is a terrible story, Coach. But why don't you just come up with some new plays?"*

> Coach Klein: *"I try. I can't. I guess I have a mental block; you know, ever since Red took my playbook and my manhood."*

In real life there have been any number of scandals involving stolen or otherwise misappropriated playbooks, especially in college football. One cannot help but think of Wake Forest's #WakeyLeaks troubles, or the infamous Tennessee/Florida rivalry shocker in 1991, or Alabama's defeat of Georgia in January of 2018, just a few days after their own playbook had been stolen. These things happen because playbooks do matter.

One of Bill Walsh's most enduring contributions to football was his popularization of the West Coast offense, which relied more on passing than on running. His playbook opened up options by trading on the unexpected, and the approach is frankly more interesting and more exciting to watch. But it was underpinned by all of the basic skills of football honed to perfection by practice, and more practice, and more practice under the watchful eye of expert coaches.

In this chapter I'll share a few trade secrets from my own tactical sales playbook, including some unbeatable plays for building bridges over the gaps in the buyer's journey.

Understanding why people buy

The core of any selling system is a right understanding of why people buy.

> *"My best friend in any account is someone with a problem I can fix."*
> *— from Miller-Heiman's "Strategic Selling"*

People change because they are dissatisfied with the status quo. The three most common versions of dissatisfaction are:

1. **Problem**—Something I'm currently experiencing, don't like, and want to get away from.

2. **Prevention**—A future problem I want to avoid.

3. **Aspiration**—A future state that I perceive to be better than my existing state.

Of the three, most salespeople would consider a current problem to be the most compelling and the most common reason for buying.

However, entire industries are based on the idea that people will make changes and investments to mitigate fear (insurance, Y2K, disaster recovery and off-site backup, etc.).

Some people will also make personal sacrifices and spend money to attain a gain or reach a goal. As a case in point, I wanted washboard abs. I did crunches and sit ups like mad. I finally got frustrated and sought advice from the guy who owns my gym. He said, "Steve, I've seen you work out. You work hard and I'll bet you have washboard abs. You just have a little laundry on the washboard!"

Experience indicates that your best customers are often those who are proactive, future-oriented, and motivated by a desire to attain a better state.

Dissatisfaction seeking missile

To succeed, an entrepreneur-cum-salesperson must become a dissatisfaction seeking missile. Figure out what dissatisfaction you can fix with your solution. Then figure out who might have that dissatisfaction. If you cannot clearly state the dissatisfaction your product or service addresses, and who might have it, then you may not have a legitimate product or service; yours may just be a solution in search of a problem. And that's not viable.

People buy because of dissatisfaction, not because of solutions. Abdominizers don't really work, but people do want to lose their bellies. So they buy them. Canadian chiropractor (and inventor) Dennis Colonello sold six million of them, on infomercials. Diet and weight-loss is a multi-billion-dollar industry.

> **Steve's Rule of Market Viability**
>
> The size of markets depends, not on the elegance of the solutions that are available, but on the dissatisfaction that is their basis.

Why buyers inadvertently thwart themselves

Selling is counterintuitive because the natural buyer goes about buying in a manner that is not well suited to the task. And the natural seller, as we have all experienced, sometimes goes about selling in an off-putting way. The default buying process is therefore a perfect storm of dysfunction.

The natural buyer avoids or rushes diagnosis and moves to solutions too quickly.

"Few of us enjoy asking for help. As research in neuroscience and psychology shows, the social threats involved—the uncertainty, risk of rejection, potential for diminished status, and inherent relinquishing of autonomy—activate the same brain regions that physical pain does. And in the workplace, where we're typically keen to demonstrate as much expertise, competence, and confidence as possible, it can feel particularly uncomfortable to make such requests. However, it's virtually impossible to advance in modern organizations without assistance from others." — Heidi Grant, "How to Get the Help You Need," Harvard Business Review *May-June 2018.*

Sellers who understand these issues can be better prepared to deal with them. These self-aware sellers can help a buyer properly understand, for example, the value of accurate diagnosis (thereby earning trust) and can also then help to achieve the right diagnosis. Eighty percent of solving a problem—in any field of endeavor—is understanding it. Moreover, a good diagnosis shapes the requirement.

A sales VP in Europe recently asked me, "How can we drive the sale versus being driven?"

There are nine principles of war according to Carl von Clausewitz in his seminal treatise *On War*. He was the father of the Prussian general staff and is still studied and relevant today. These principles of war are actually more universal; they are general principles of strategy.

One of the nine principles is "The offensive—to seize and maintain the initiative." It is the same as "to drive the sale versus being driven." A mutual agenda at the beginning of every sales call is designed to seize the initiative. The diagnostic questioning process helps the salesperson maintain the initiative. Unlike war, this serves the best interest of both parties.

Unfortunately, as I mentioned, sellers are often complicit in a dysfunctional buying process. The confluence of uncorrected natural (i.e., suboptimal) buyer and seller behaviors predictably results in the most common sales error: Premature presentations. That is to say, prescription without diagnosis. From the seller's side, this is driven by two issues:

1. We are human and fear conflict, so we naturally seek to avoid asking the hard questions.

2. We firmly believe that a polished presentation will be sufficiently persuasive to win the day, because we think that buying is primarily an intellectual decision. It is not. It is primarily emotional, no matter what anyone says.

Back to the Buyer's Journey

Let's now return to the buyer's journey and take a more in-depth look at it, paying special attention to the gaps along the way.

The Buyer's Journey

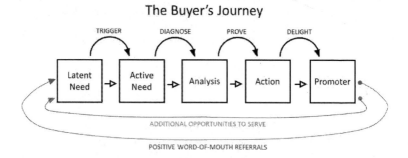

We'll consult my own tactical sales playbook for some insight into how sellers properly bridge the gaps. Success depends on executing excellent plays in the right situations at the right time. There really is a best way to guide a buyer along his journey.

The perfect trigger conversation

From the seller's perspective, the trigger conversation is the first engagement with the buyer; it's the first play of the game; it's the opening kickoff. It sets the tone. It's an important call. I'll describe the perfect trigger call structure in sufficient detail to allow you to plan,

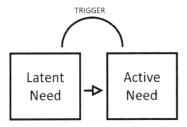

conduct, and critique your own trigger calls. The trigger call is an unscheduled call. It is an interruption; a surprise; a call out of the blue. It may be a cold call. It may be a lead follow-up call. But from the buyer's perspective, it is unexpected.

If it's a cold call, it is designed to be the trigger event that takes the buyer from latent need to active need. In this case the buyer has expressed no prior interest.

If it's a lead follow-up, the buyer has downloaded a free version of your software, attended a webinar, or taken some other positive action that signals some sort of interest.

Incidentally, cold calling does not necessarily need to be part of your overall selling process. In Chapter 13, Mind the Gap, I'll provide a universal list of lead generation mechanisms, any of which can be done either by the sales team, or by the marketing team. The key is that your sales/marketing process has to start at the beginning. There has to be some way to generate leads to fill the sales funnel.

For most companies, big and small, old and new, lack of leads is the bottleneck that constrains revenue. A trickle here means a trickle everywhere past this point.

Even for those (lucky few) who have plenty of solid leads, being the trigger that moves a prospect from latent need to active need will always put you at a competitive advantage. Just as with baby birds, there is a primacy effect. A baby bird imprints on the first creature it sees when it breaks out of the shell. Buyers imprint on the diagnostician who takes them from latent to active need.

In addition, if you're the one who initiates contact, you get to choose the entry point. The more senior the initial contact

- the shorter the sales cycle, and
- the higher the margin

We'll cover entry points in more detail in the sales strategy playbook in the next chapter. In the meantime, let's take a look at the perfect trigger call. In my playbook, the perfect trigger call is a seven step process. Each step offers a principle, a method for correctly applying the principle, and precise stage direction for how to deliver the message each step of the way.

The chart below will give you a general overview of just exactly what a perfect trigger call might look like. After that we'll dig more deeply into each step.

The Perfect Trigger Call

Principle	Method	Vocal Persona
1. Cognitive Mobilizer	*Hi, this is Steve Kraner. Did I get you at a bad time?*	Concerned
Eliminate the Heisman		
2. Disarming Honesty	*It sounds like you have figured this out. As I said, my name is Steve Kraner, with Software Sales Gurus, and this is a sales call. Are you sure you don't want to hang up?*	Playful
Establish Trust		
3. Proposed Plan	*I appreciate your courtesy. John, bottom line is I don't know whether we have anything for you but, with your permission, I'll ask for three minutes to give you the top three reasons a CEO of a software company could be interested in carving out time to talk to me. If one of them makes sense you can invite me to talk with you further. If not, I'm out of your hair. If I stick to the three minutes, do I have your permission?*	Even Pace
Mutual Goal		

4. Precision Probes	*When I speak to your colleagues—other CEO's of software companies—they say their sales team is solid but the sales forecast is not always as accurate as they'd like. I don't assume you see that in your organization, though?*	Mirror
Identify a Potential Need		
5. Deeper Diagnostic	*I just called in out of the blue, and this is a sensitive area, so without going too far, is there anything additional you think I should understand about your organization?*	Mirror
Diagnose Urgency		
6. Call to Action: Next Step or No	*We are at the three-minute mark. If I told you, we help in this area, would you want to carve out more time to explore this further? Or should we pull the plug?*	Mirror
Next Step or No		
7. Confront Cognitive Dissonance	*I'm looking forward to meeting you. Are you sure it's worth carving out an hour to explore this further, or did I push you into this meeting?*	Mirror
Reaffirm Commitment		

Step 1: Cognitive mobilizer

As I write this, my dear wife Judy just arrived at the Marriott Residence Inn where we're staying while our house is being remodeled. She told me that when she left the gym she drove straight to our house, as if on auto-pilot, instead of driving here to the hotel as she'd intended.

In his book *Thinking Fast and Slow,* Daniel Kahneman explains the brain science behind this behavior. It applies to everyone.

Like a smart phone display, the human brain is switched off most of the time. Both the phone and the brain do that for the same reason: To conserve energy. Our brain, when fully engaged, uses more calories than any other organ in our body. And so, as a survival adaptation, we respond to most stimuli with standard, non-thinking responses. This is "thinking fast." It is a rule-based, non-thoughtful, standard response to standard stimuli.

Let's illustrate with a thought role-play. Imagine you're the buyer in a store and the shopkeeper comes up to you and says, "Can I help you?"

How do you respond?

I've done that role-pay with random people thousands of times. The standard, non-thoughtful response to the approach of a salesperson is, "No thanks. Just looking." I call it the Heisman. It's an automatic response to stiff-arm the seller.

Have you ever stiff-armed a shopkeeper and then, even though you could use some help, you're now reluctant to ask for it?

If you're making unscheduled outbound calls, you're like the shopkeeper. You're initially a nuisance and you are to be avoided. You get the Heisman. Baseline measurement, before training, shows most salespeople making cold calls are getting stiff-armed 95% of the time.

The Cognitive Mobilizer is designed to reduce this to 5%. And it's really simple. Standard sales stimulus usually looks something like this:

- "Hi, this is Kevin Kold from AppMajic. How are you today?" (said with excessive enthusiasm) or
- "Just reaching out…" or

- "Who is your VP of Development?" (not even a name, just a title)

People on the receiving end of these kinds of calls don't think, they react. Almost always negatively. In order to change the reaction, you have to change the way you open the conversation. Instead of a standard stimulus, present a cognitive difficulty (a novel stimulus for which there is no standard, non-thinking, rule-based response like the Heisman).

As you saw in the chart above, I suggest: "Hi, this is Steve Kraner. Did I get you at a bad time?" (Concerned.)

Measure this yourself. Done right, in a concerned tone, it reduces the Heisman to 5%. And it causes the buyer's brain to engage.

And by the way, do not be alarmed or put off if they gruffly say, "It's never a great time. What do you want?" That's a common and perfectly reasonable answer. It is NOT the Heisman. Just move on.

Step 2: Disarming honesty

My mentor in the sales training world taught me to use a "pretense call." It involved lying to the buyer by suggesting that I had gotten a message which said the buyer had called me. As a West Point graduate, having lived under the cadet honor code, I could not bring myself to lie. I decided to try the opposite. Instead of trying to be devious, I am clear and direct: "It sounds like you have figured this out. As I said, my name is Steve Kraner, with Software Sales Gurus, and this is a sales call. Are you sure you don't want to hang up?" (Playful.)

Ben Damm, who learned about disarming honesty at Oracle, said few of the people who were taught that technique used it. But he did and it worked.

I'm well aware that most people I've coached to practice such forthrightness never actually do try it. Pride and fear tend to keep them from even giving it a shot. Those brave enough to try have discovered, like Ben, that it causes most buyers to laugh. And if you've never experienced a genuinely amused buyer on a cold call, you're missing out. And your calls have probably been a bit like running your car without enough oil. Add some disarming honesty; it's like adding lubrication to an engine.

The compliment metric

I love data. Here's an astonishing bit of data (which, incidentally, I would not have believed if I had not measured it for myself in several organizations): If you perform your outbound calls well, one out of five buyers will compliment you on your call performance. Seriously. If you're not getting actual compliments 20% of the time, try a change. After all, it's a testable proposition. (I mention this "compliment metric" here because disarming honesty plays a measurable role in good call performance.)

> *Note – the third column in the summing up chart provides stage direction and for Step 2 says "Playful." If you sound "Freaked Out" it will not work.*

In the case of a lead follow-up call, you might say: "Sounds like I may have caught you unaware. We spoke briefly about our solutions at the XYX conference and this is the dreaded sales follow-up call—are you sure you don't want to hang up?" (Playful.)

Step 3: Proposed plan

Since this call is all our idea (and a surprise to the buyer), we cannot use the preferred mutual agenda for the call. Instead, we substitute a proposed plan.

You may have noticed in the perfect trigger call chart above that the stage direction for the proposed plan (on a cold call) is: "Even pace." Since there are a lot of words, we tend to rush. Slow down. Rushed sounds desperate. An even pace provides a sense that you are comfortable in your own skin; you have gravitas.

For a lead follow-up, try: "I appreciate your courtesy. With your permission, I'll ask for three minutes to get a sense of your interest or lack thereof. If it makes sense, we can figure out how to keep in touch. If not, I'm out of your hair. I can make sure we are not crossing that fine line between persistence and stalking, up to and including deleting your name from our database. If I stick to the three minutes, do I have your permission?"

Step 4: Precision probes

For a cold call, I suggest that you prepare three precision probes. You saw an example in the chart. I'll also provide you with my handy capabilities translator to help.

For a lead follow-up call, by contrast, because they somehow expressed interest, use an open diagnostic question. For example: "Most people I call don't remember signing up for the webinar and suspect that I am fabricating that. Do you remember signing up, or is that what you're thinking, too?"

NOTE: Since so many say they don't recall registering, or didn't attend, or didn't read the whitepaper, it helps if you defuse that by saying it first and making a bit of fun of yourself in the process.

You might also try something like: "What inspired you to register? Did you participate in a webinar, download the white paper, stop by our booth, or was it merely an impulse that passed?"

If they respond, proceed to need diagnostic questions. If they don't, the call may be over.

Step 5: Deeper diagnostic

On an unscheduled outbound call, with a (self-imposed) three-minute limit, you will not be able to ask too many need diagnostic questions. You might get one, two, or maybe three. When you hit the three-minute limit, you must stop and move on to Step 6.

Before we move on, I must share a key point about nuances in how you ask questions. When you are prospecting, it is critical that you have a soft entry into the diagnostic. This is a well-documented case of the importance of subtle differences in language that make or break.

If you say, "Can you tell me more?" or worse, "Tell me more" (a command) it will very likely cause them to shut down.

If you modify that to say, "I called in out of the blue and cyber security is a sensitive area. Without going too far, is there additional insight you think I should understand?" it will in all likelihood lower their defenses.

I use the cyber example because I have had the honor to work with a number of cybersecurity firms. As a rule, the salespeople are certain you can't ask a cybersecurity professional to talk about cyber risk on a cold call because it is too sensitive. You could be a hacker. These well-intended cyber salespeople are wrong and I have the game film to prove it.

But they are on to the point I just made above. ALL buyers—not just cyber security people—are like deer entering a clearing at this point. They are on edge and ready to bolt at the slightest alarm.

A soft entry usually makes it work.

From this point on, the process is identical for cold calls and lead follow up calls.

Step 6: Call to action – next step or no

At three minutes, you should stop the conversation and say: "We are at the three-minute mark. If I told you we have solutions in this area, would you want to carve out more time to explore this further? Or should we pull the plug?"

You will get a lot of noes, but that goes with the territory. If you have done it well, you will leave a positive impression even if you get a no.

Your goal should not be to get an appointment, even if you are paid by appointment. Your goal should be to either find dissatisfaction or be told no.

Jen Zahos, who started as a young sales development rep, has moved up rapidly and has held senior positions at places like Symantec, Veritas, and Pure Storage. She told me that prior to using the trigger call her goal on a call was either:

Plan A: Get an appointment, or failing that, resort to
Plan B: Send literature and follow up.

After the training, she said she approached calls with one goal: Either uncover a problem she could fix or get a conclusive no.

This subtle shift in direction changes your mindset going into a call, and improves your performance.

For those whose dissatisfaction is triggered, they will want to proceed. They may want to take more time immediately. If they do, just continue down the need diagnostic. If they want to set a future appointment, move on to Step 7.

Step 7: Confront cognitive dissonance

Sometimes leads actually ARE weak. If you've done much prospecting, you know that there is a "no-show" rate for appointments. You may not be aware that the no-show rate is directly related to the application of pressure: The more prospects feel pressured, the higher the no-show rate rises.

A client once asked me to look into "bad leads" in his organization. I agreed to do so, and spent a day riding with one of his salespeople who was following up three leads. The first was at a doctor's office. Upon arrival we discovered the door was locked and the office was closed. The doctor was not in.

As we approached the second location the salesperson saw a man darting from the office to his truck. Like a bounty hunter, my intrepid salesperson sprang from his car and caught up with the man. To his credit, he got the guy to sit down and talk. The man had intended to be gone, but was just a bit late.

At the third location we knocked. No one answered.

When I went to the call center, I found unskilled young people under immense pressure to produce appointments. Nearly all the appointments were with people who could only manage to get these desperate reps off the phone by agreeing to an appointment. They never had any intention of keeping it.

If your goal is to set high quality appointments, then focus on the dissatisfaction and not on getting the appointment. And let the prospect off the hook before you hang up. Few things are 100%, but I have never heard a buyer back out of an appointment at this point. Graciously offering them the freedom to back out minimizes the no-show rate. The offer shows that you value the person more than a transaction. And you have accelerated the onset of cognitive dissonance (or buyer's remorse) so that it has been resolved in their mind.

By doing this you are able to:

- Create consistent good impressions in the market, even with people who said no.
- Set a high-quality appointment, based on an identified need.

Remember marketing 101. It takes, on average, seven positive impressions before a customer does business with you. Familiarity is the first hurdle.

If you create a bad impression, it takes ten positive impressions to overcome it.

If you do not consciously work to provide this level of prescriptive instruction, you are likely to unconsciously revert to old and ineffective habits, including pressure or even trickery.

If you are using a freemium model, it's very easy to burn out your list if you use a process that creates negative impressions.

The Capability Translator

In a moment I will provide you with a sales tool called the Capability Translator. You can use it to craft role-specific diagnostic probes. The example I've included was developed for a client who wants to sell credit card processing services that are tied to contacts in Salesforce. In this case they target Salesforce resellers who will offer this as an add-on to their clients. But first, there are two primary cold calling principles employed that we have not yet discussed.

1. **Narrowcast versus broadcast.** Marketing messages are often designed for one-way mass communication to a broad audience. Broadcasting, as it is known (or scattering widely, or shotgunning), is an effective way to sell simple products like headache remedies and toothpaste and laundry detergent. It can also be extremely effective for building brands and/or product familiarity because broadcast messages can be specifically tailored to create positive impressions in the marketplace. Think of the gecko. Or the duck. I'd venture to guess that most people couldn't quite say what AFLAC does, but I'd bet they know the duck.

   But broadcasting messages tend to lose validity and impact when you get to the individual level. There is no family of 2.5 people. Gerald Weinberg, in his book *The Secrets of Consulting*, proposed the Raspberry Jam Rule of marketing: the further you spread it, the thinner it gets.

   It's not typically the job of a salesperson to create brand or product awareness; such efforts are lead generators and are usually best handled by the marketing wizards. Instead, salespeople deal with people one-on-one, which also has distinct advantages. If slogans (or strange-but-adorable wildlife) could sell complex solutions, we wouldn't need salespeople.

   Narrowcast (or individualized, specifically tailored) questions are the purview of the salesperson. Diagnostic questions should be crafted such that they create a sense of an insider understanding of *this particular person's* world.

2. **Language of the problem set.** Marketing messages may be based on language of the solution set (i.e., Ultra Luster Car Wax) or language of the problem set (eliminates swirl marks). Language of the solution set is not the language customers speak and it comes across as hyperbole.

Salespeople must be able to describe a problem or aspiration that a particular buyer might have in language that the buyer speaks and understands in order for the message to resonate.

How to prepare for a cold call campaign

I suggest the following simple (if not always easy) steps to prepare for a cold call campaign:

- Organize your calls into campaigns aimed at a single vertical market, title, and solution.
- Prepare three role-specific diagnostic questions, using the Capability Translator.
- Research before you call so that you are fully prepared.
- Then, when actually sitting down to dial the phone, take the advice of the marketing stars at Nike: Just do it.

If you are following up on leads:

- Get whatever insight you can from the lead.
- Take some time to research the individual you will be calling, and also the company where he works. Start with your CRM, and if absolutely necessary, check online. Gaining some cursory insight into your potential buyers and their needs is always useful—but I don't need to remind you that noodling around the web can be a serious time drain.

Now let's take a look at the Capability Translator (to download the Capability Translator and other tools that will be mentioned as we go along, please go to www.softwaresalesgurus.com, click the "Sales Tips" tab, then the "Coaching Toolbox" tab and use the password "goodselling").

Capability Translator

1. Pick a product or service
2. Describe a key feature
3. Pick a title of a person you want to meet
4. Pick a vertical market, profession or government agency
5. Describe a benefit that applies to this person
6. Describe differentiator that makes your solution better
7. Enter the persona's problem or aspiration, to which your differentiator is the solution.
8. Create a link from the KNOWN to the NEW.
9. Create a paradoxical intent question to reveal the need.

Your Solution	Target Persona
1. Your Product/Service: *Credit card processing tied into Salesforce*	**3. Target Title:** *President or owner of a Salesforce reseller*
2. Key Feature: *Credit card processing that is linked directly to contacts*	**4. Target Vertical:** *Salesforce resellers/CRM consultants*
5. Benefit to this persona: *Solidify relationships with existing clients by offering another business solution. The more value you provide the greater the chance of renewal. The more ways you are tied to a customer, the harder it is for them to get rid of you.*	**7. Problem or Aspiration** **Problem:** *Customers who do not renew their Salesforce agreements.* **Aspiration:** *New ways to give account managers or customer success managers guidance to proactively do things to make renewals happen.*
6. Differentiator: *Easier to deploy* **8. Link the new to the known:** *In banking, if a customer has five accounts they are a customer for life.*	**9. Paradoxical intent question:** *In the banking industry, if a client has multiple types of accounts with a bank, they are unlikely to leave. I know you guys are always a step ahead. Would adding credit card processing help lock in your Salesforce customers – or are you satisfied with your current Salesforce renewal rates?*

So there we have the perfect trigger call structure, which gives you the tools to plan, conduct, and critique a—dare I say perfect?— trigger call.

And the Capability Translator provides a way for marketing or sales to create targeted messages (that is to say, precision probes), in an orderly fashion.

Now we'll turn out attention to the perfect discovery call. But before we do, let me reassure you that although this is primarily a how-to book for CEOs to build a sales team, I will nevertheless address the need for a strategic marketing process in Chapter 12, Strategic Marketing. It's an essential element for strategic growth, and in fact it really ought to precede both the creation/adoption of the selling system and the building of a sales team. And in Chapter 13, Mind the Gap, I'll provide a more comprehensive treatment of lead generation and the sales and marketing interface.

The perfect discovery call

The core of persuasion is "tripping over the truth" as Chip and Dan Heath describe in their latest 2017 best seller, *The Power of Moments: Why Certain Experiences have Extraordinary Impact.* Tripping over the truth is not comfortable. It may be agonizing. It is often a sudden realization of a deep and meaningful truth. It can be gut wrenching. And it is absolutely required for someone to want to change.

A person may trip over the truth by accident. It does happen sometimes. But it can also be orchestrated; we can create opportunities to help people (or nudge them slightly) to trip over the truth. Chapter 5 of *The Power of Moments* includes a vivid description of the Community-led total sanitation (CLTS) process used in developing countries to persuade villagers to use latrines (instead of disassembling them to sell for parts). The key is to demonstrate a compelling reason to change behavior, so they *want* to use the latrine for its intended purpose. You can provide as much hardware as you want; unless there is a very good reason to change behavior it is so much scrap material.

CLTS is just a recent incarnation of something embedded in every effective sales process: A method to cause a buyer to trip over the truth.

Neil Rackham was the first to uncover and systematically document what he described as the SPIN process (Situation – Problem – Implication – Need/Payoff), which is a structured questioning process designed to, as the Heath brothers so eloquently put it, "crystalize dissatisfaction."

Strategic sales processes recognize crystalized dissatisfaction as the basis of every opportunity. Miller-Heiman, as I mentioned, says: "My best friend in any account is someone with a problem I can solve." Target Account Selling refers to a compelling event. These processes, because they focus on sales only at the strategic level, do not offer the tactical tools to crystalize dissatisfaction.

Every tactical selling system has at its core a structured questioning process to facilitate tripping over the truth and crystalizing dissatisfaction. The first was SPIN. Solution Selling uses the Nine Boxes. Sandler uses a proprietary Pain Funnel[SM].

More current evidence of the importance of uncovering dissatisfaction shows up in current research by Gong.io. Gong offers cloud-based conversation management. They are one of several new competitive offerings in this emerging area who provide sales call recording and coaching solutions. They say they use machine learning to analyze their large database of buyer/seller conversations and are able to assess them based on win/loss data.

Not surprisingly, Gong concludes that highly successful salespeople hold different conversations than their average peers. I find their dashboard to be a nice upgrade to standard recording technology. I have also solicited input from my clients who use their services, including top-performing salespeople. They value the data that Gong.io provides about what top performers do differently than their peers. Examples include:

- Successful sellers ask more questions than their peers. Gong says 14 more. My observation indicates this number can and should be higher. But we agree on more questions.

- Even during a demo, successful sellers have conversation switches every 76 seconds. (Gong loves to give very exact numbers.)
- 60/40 talk ratio. Again, we are in the same ball park but my human observation indicates the very best salespeople on the planet are at 90/10 (salesperson doing 10% of the talking) in the best discovery calls.
- In successful sales conversations pricing is discussed at the 45-minute mark. This is a good indicator of WHAT to do. In terms of HOW to do it, my own research confirms that you can talk about the price too early or too late, and that 45-minutes into a 60-minute conversation is about the right time. There is, of course, also a specific process that is occupying this time, which I will describe presently.

Data reported by Alison Wood Brooks and Leslie John in an article entitled, "The Surprising Power of Questions" (*Harvard Business Review*, May-June 2018) takes this principle to the next level of specificity. Brooks and John did research that suggests there are four keys to effective questioning. They point out that the best questioning technique depends on your purpose. What is effective for a journalist is not necessarily effective for a salesperson or a police investigator. There are four factors they describe for effective questioning:

1. **Framing**
2. **Type**
3. **Sequence**
4. **Tone**

My years of research and observation, especially listening to sales game film and live sales interactions, indicate that a question asked in one way will result in a buyer who shuts down, but when the same question is asked in a subtly different way, the buyer willingly engages. Nuances matter. Throughout this section I will point out questions that consistently lead to resistance and questions that result in willing engagement.

In sales, it is easy to go wrong. It's a balancing act. Your goal is to build a relationship. But it's more complex. You need to cause someone to "trip over the truth" without injuring their self-esteem. I listen to a lot of sales game film and hear salespeople trying to "challenge" the buyer. In the process, they are far more likely to offend than persuade.

Let's take a look at the nuances of questioning in the context of a sales call that make the difference.

Framing means properly setting expectations at the beginning of the conversation. The Perfect Discovery Call Checklist is a tool to help you structure a scheduled diagnostic or discovery call (to download the Perfect Discovery Call Checklist, please go to www.softwaresalesgurus.com, click the "Sales Tips" tab, then the "Coaching Toolbox" tab and use the password "goodselling").

The Perfect Discovery Call Checklist				
Company: Buyer Name: Role: Salesperson:	Notes	Accusatory	Pushed	Broke Trust
Mutual Agenda				
☐ Timeframe				
☐ Buyer(s) goal for this call				
☐ Premise for seller questions				
☐ No Go (thick skin)				
☐ Go (last five minutes)				
Need Diagnostic				
☐ Role-specific probe (if needed)				
☐ Further insight?				
☐ Other details?				
☐ Specific instance?				
☐ How long has this been on your radar?				
☐ Past efforts?				
☐ Significant progress?				

☐ Big picture impact is minimal?				
☐ Difficult to quantify $?				
☐ Buyer priority?				
☐ Reason for priority?				
Buyer's Utopian Vision				
☐ Customer's baby				
☐ Unique fit				
☐ Deal with no fit				
Dealing with Money				
☐ Explain Pricing Model				
☐ Solid number on table				
☐ With confidence				
☐ "No drip" mobile defense				
Mutual Action Plan				
☐ When is the latest?				
☐ Past, similar process?				
☐ No one else cares?				
☐ Co-built				
☐ Clear steps defined				
☐ Let them know you will send it in writing for review				

The perfect discovery call is a scheduled call. It is not unannounced. It does not take the prospective buyer by surprise.

Mutual agenda

The perfect discovery call opens with the establishment of a mutual agenda. Each element of the agenda is proposed in the form of a question and we seek the buyer's agreement. The seller:

- Confirms the timeframe for the conversation
- Asks or confirms the buyer's goals for the conversation
- Establishes a mutually beneficial reason for why the seller should begin with questions

- Allows for the buyer to say "no" at the end, ensuring this conflict-laden moment will be anxiety-free
- Allows five minutes at the end to plan next steps, if the answer was not "no."

This structure has been developed through years of split testing, recording, analyzing, and improving the sales process.

A quick aside

I'll just take a moment to share with you a typical example of my current experimentation. As I write this in late 2018, I'm conducting a split test with Black Duck Software. Black Duck is led by a serial entrepreneur named Lou Shipley, who also leads the sales curricula both at Harvard and at the MIT Sloan School of Management.

The sales team at Black Duck is led by Adam Clay, a serial sales team builder. He and his team of "golden goose trainers" (his first line sales managers) produce quite possibly the best salespeople on the planet.

Together, Lou and Adam have led Black Duck through 14 consecutive quarters of record growth. Not long ago Black Duck was purchased by Synopsys for $548M, a multiple of seven. Synopsys said they paid that premium for:

- Technology (Bill Ledingham's tech is the best), and
- Sales process

In this experiment, we've modified the third element of the mutual agenda to offer the buyer an option:

A. Begin with an overview of the seller's offering
B. Begin by asking questions to get a deeper understanding of the buyer and her goal

What do you think most buyers choose?

Years of experimenting have proven that what we think is going to happen and what *does* happen are often two different things. Moreover, what we think is the cause of our success (or failure) and what actually *is* the cause of our success (or failure) are rarely in sync.

That's why it's no accident that the first selling system was developed by a third-party observer, John Patterson's brother-in-law. It's why there's immense value in behavioral psychologist Neil Rackham's 12 years of third-party observation of Xerox salespeople. It's why Gong's database of recorded sales calls provides extraordinary insight into what leads to wins and losses. And it's why there's great merit in the work of researchers like Brooks and John on effective questioning.

It's also why there's enormous risk associated with the unverified teachings of so many sales training programs. Most sales techniques have no basis in research, which is why they so often blow up in the faces of the salespeople who dutifully employ them.

In our ongoing, current sales experiment with Black Duck, the relatively small data set so far indicates:

- 100% of salespeople and sales leaders say that buyers want option A, an overview. (I have asked 348 salespeople and leaders to date.)
- 94.2% (147 of 156, two months into the experiment) of buyers prefer option B, the questions. They frequently say, "Why don't I give you an overview of what we're looking for and then you can ask questions?"

It seems the majority of buyers are willing to participate in a diagnostic, while the majority of sellers think buyers want a pitch.

My purpose in sharing this early data is to impact your current beliefs. As you will discover in the Sales Star Model (in Chapter 10), your actions are merely a manifestation of your current beliefs. If we change a (wrong) belief, right behavior follows with it. And the change can be made permanent.

Back to framing, et. al.

Having properly *framed* why we are asking questions and gained the buyer's willing participation using a mutual agenda, let's now consider some important nuances regarding *type*, *sequence*, and *tone* of sales questioning.

Type of question is a well-worn (maybe even threadbare) topic in sales training. Unfortunately, what is most widely repeated and accepted is just plain wrong. In their studies, Brooks and John debunk old school ideas that have been passed on for generations by sales trainers.

The idea, for example, that we should favor open-ended questions over closed questions does not have a solid basis in fact. In fairness, Rackham pointed that out 30 years ago, too. When I ask salespeople what they know about asking good questions, they often say, "Open-ended questions are best!" They are repeating sales myths.

The Brooks and John studies suggest that the best type of question is a follow-up question. While their studies in this area were not focused on questioning in a sales role *per se*, the best sales processes agree with the findings, and employ follow-up questions. Buyers appreciate follow-up questions because they show that the seller is listening.

For sales, we need to put a much finer point on the purpose of our follow-up questions. Follow-up questions encourage the contemplation of consequences, which causes a buyer to advance the cycle of awareness.

Another short diversion

My nature is to be a geek and that means really needing to know the why behind the what. I know not everyone will share that (compulsive) need. My goal in referencing multiple sciences and sources, decades old to current, is to demonstrate that, as in accounting, the columns all add up to the same sum. So we have confidence in the result.

Let's do a quick review of some decades old, proven, and useful science.

Gestalt cycle of experience and the buyer's journey

Before we can understand the necessity for a structured process for need diagnosis, we must understand the human cycle of awareness.

Accepted psychology aligns with a modern sales process which aligns with new brain science which aligns with common modern marketing's portrayal of the buyer's journey.

Ph.D.'s please forgive my simplistic treatment. I am a layperson.

The Gestalt model starts with the idea that organisms seek to achieve and maintain a stable state; i.e., rest. They will experience disrupters from internal needs, like hunger. As they interact with their environment, they will also experience external disruptors, like predators. But the organism seeks to get back to rest by the shortest path possible.

The Gestalt Cycle of Experience

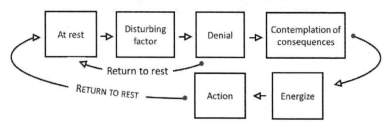

The basic cycle of experience can be described in seven steps:

1. **At rest.** I am sleeping at 3 a.m.

2. **Disturbing factor.** I hear a sound in my dream. I awake and wonder if the sound is real.

3. **Denial.** The quickest way to get back to steady state is to deny a problem. If I wake up in the middle of the night and think I hear a sound, it is very likely I will convince myself it is nothing and go back to sleep. Most awareness cycles stop here and few proceed. We want to get back to rest, even if we are not asleep.

4. **Contemplation of consequences**. If I move past sensing and denial to contemplation of consequences, however, the cycle may advance. If I achieve intellectual awareness it occurs to me that perhaps the sound is real. Perhaps it's a cell phone that is running out of power. But perhaps it's a carbon monoxide detector and we are in danger.

5. **Energize.** I have an instant burning desire to act. My amygdala (the fight-flight-freeze center of my brain) fires up.

6. **Action.** I get up and walk through the house to identify the source of the sound. I search and find that Verizon installed a large battery backup and that when the battery no longer charges, it sounds an alarm. I remove the battery and the alarm stops.

7. **Return to rest.** I go back to sleep.

Need diagnostic

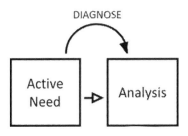

Let's take a moment to have a closer look at the need diagnostic section of the perfect discovery call. You may have noticed above that all of the questions asked in this part of the call (with the possible exception of the first) are follow-up questions that are specifically intended to facilitate the contemplation of consequences (Step 4 of the Gestalt model) and to crystalize dissatisfaction to the point where action ensues (Step 5 of the same). Here's the section in question:

Need Diagnostic			
☐ Role-specific probe (if needed)			
☐ Further insight?			
☐ Other details?			
☐ Specific instance?			
☐ How long has this been on your radar?			

☐ Past efforts?				
☐ Significant progress?				
☐ Big picture impact is minimal?				
☐ Difficult to quantify $?				
☐ Buyer priority?				
☐ Reason for priority?				

Note that I said the questions are intended to facilitate, not force. If this process yields action as a natural outcome, that is good for both parties. On the other hand, if after a serious, honest, and focused contemplation of the consequences the conclusion is that action is not compelled, that is also good. It is always best for all involved to get all of the truth out in the open as quickly and smoothly as possible.

The first question, which I've labelled the role-specific probe, is normally not needed because buyers almost always put their problem or aspiration on the table when you ask their goal for the conversation. If they don't, then you will need to ask an open or role-specific diagnostic probe.

Brooks and John mention that buyers are more willing to give honest answers if they have an "out." For sales conversations, I'd again like to put a much finer point on that (even at risk of making a very different point than they intended; so blame me, not them, if this is hard to swallow): I'd recommend an anti-suggestion.

Anti-suggestions are my favorite type of question for getting straight to the crux. The basis for anti-suggestions is the Law of Paradoxical Intent:

If you're desperate to make something happen, and you try to control events and people, you push away the very people you want to influence and you prevent the outcome you seek.

The term "anti-suggestion" actually comes from psychotherapy. As a general rule of thumb, therapists are taught not to make suggestions for the simple reason that patients will tend to fight against them, often with detrimental or even perilous consequences.

Consider, for example, the following interaction in an imperfect therapy session:

Therapist: *"Maybe you should consider rehab."*
Patient: *"I don't want rehab. I don't need rehab. I won't go."*

This push-back is called "reactance."

It happens in sales just as it does in therapy, and in every other instance of human relations for that matter.

Consider, for example, the sales tactic known as the "tie-down." It sounds something like this:

Salesperson: *"Wouldn't you agree, Mr. Buyer, that if we could show you a 20% saving you should act?"*

It rarely (if ever) produces the desired response. It sounds a bit manipulative, maybe desperate. It creates resistance. The unintended (and undesirable) result is reactance:

Buyer: *"Well, not necessarily. Actually, no, I wouldn't agree at all."*

If you try to tie a buyer down, you will not gain agreement. You will create resistance.

But the inverse is also true. The anti-suggestion is the opposite of the tie-down and it has the opposite effect. Reactance works regardless of the direction. If you pull in they will push away; if you push away, they will pull in. If you try to talk them out of it, they begin to talk themselves into it. This is the reason that what most of us call reverse psychology works.

Suppose I suggest, in a sales context, "Perhaps doing nothing is your best option?" The buyer's subconscious mind will begin to think: Steve doesn't sound like he needs my business. Steve must be doing well. Steve must have good stuff.

If I appear skeptical and I ask, "How will you justify the cost of a solution just for your group?" The buyer replies, "Well, it's justified because ...."

If I graciously offer to exit, more often than not the buyer will try to keep me engaged. This creates a role-reversal. The buyer is convincing the seller.

This powerful (if counterintuitive) conversational tactic has been available to humans since the advent of language itself. Someone once described the underlying forces thus:

> *If you state an opinion to me in a dogmatic manner, which is in direct opposition to my thought, and you imply no room to negotiate, then I must conclude, in order to protect my own self-esteem, that you are wrong and will immediately undertake to prove you are wrong. On the other hand, if you state your opinion as a hypothesis, with evidence of willingness to discuss and explore, I will most likely undertake to prove you correct.*

Note particularly the phrase "… then I must conclude, in order to protect my self-esteem, that you are wrong.…" People cannot help but defend their current idea if presented with an idea in opposition to their own because it feels like an attack on their self-esteem.

If you think in terms of the Law of Paradoxical Intent, when a salesperson tries to control a buyer's thoughts or manipulate a buyer's emotions, buyers will naturally fight to be free of any attempt to limit their liberty. Indeed, freedom will become their sole focus in the moment.

If you listen to sales calls, you'll see that this pattern is clear. Most attempts to challenge or uncover pain create resistance because they seem arrogant and accusatory. They are demeaning.

Do we really expect the buyer to be vulnerable in a threatening environment?

This advice is really speaking to a nuance of language. You can say almost anything you like, and make almost any point, if you do it in a hypothetical way and leave the buyer an easy out. That's when the magic happens. When given an option, the buyer will "… most likely undertake to prove you correct."

Why? Because humans fear conflict and we do not want to fight. If given the option, the human compulsion to avoid conflict and to be liked kicks in.

So then is the anti-suggestion manipulative? As with all sales techniques, the intent behind the technique determines its impact. I would like to suggest that if we *don't* ask questions like this we are PRESUMING, which the dictionary defines as 1) *arrogant* and 2) *guessing* (among other things not positively correlated with successful communications).

If we do not ask these questions we are presuming that:

- This buyer has a need.
- This buyer is aware of the need.
- This need is a priority to this buyer.
- Acting on this need is cost-justified in this buyer's mind.
- This need is a priority to this buyer's organization.
- Our solution will resolve this buyer's need.
- Our solution is the best solution available to this buyer.
- This need justifies action now, above other priorities.

If you make a deliberate effort not to presume these things and to embrace the likelihood of alternative possibilities, your belief will impact your demeanor, and you will signal the positive intent that makes this tactic effective.

The best anti-suggestions are not "moves" because they are 100% honest inquiries stemming from a genuine desire to make no assumptions, but rather to discover the truth.

Here are a few examples of specific anti-suggestions to help you implement this conversational sales tactic. And remember: Anti-suggestions are powerful when used with the right tone (born of honest inquiry) and dangerous when used with the wrong tone (born of unscrupulous manipulation).

When you are following up with someone who has downloaded some of your stuff, try opening the conversation with something like this:

- *Did I catch you at a bad time?* (Concerned tone), or
- *This is the dreaded sales follow-up call – do you want to hang up?* (Playful tone)

Try these questions when you are trying to gauge:

Timeframe: *You haven't mentioned any need for speed on this project. Is that because there is none?* (Tone: If you honestly believe it is possible that there is no need for speed in this specific instance, this will work like a charm. Remember, to assume a need for speed is presuming; both guessing and arrogant.)

Personal priority: *For you personally, this is not a front burner issue?* (Honest)

Organizational impact: *The impact is limited to your department?* (Honest)

Support of others: *It's not on other people's minds?* (Honest)

Financial impact and cost justification: *Building the business case will be difficult in this case?* (Honest)

Solution Fit: *So, in your eyes, our solution looks like overkill?* (Honest)

And when you are closing for the appointment, try:

Your call. Should we find a way to explore this further, or is it time to pull the plug? (Honest)

As I said, anti-suggestions create a role-reversal. The buyer convinces the seller; not the other way around.

Back again to the surprising power of questions

Sequence of questions is less well-studied in sales methodologies, although SPIN (the acronym itself, remember, is a questioning sequence), Solution Selling, and Sandler all provide a prescriptive sequence of questions. In practice, a prescribed sequence of questions can be either too prescriptive or not prescriptive enough.

The Perfect Discovery Call Checklist is designed to hit the right balance. It will appear too prescriptive to most people (as it did to me prior to experimentation). Split testing proves this is the right balance.

The value of a perfectly balanced checklist is established in *The Checklist Manifesto* by Atul Gawande that I mentioned in Chapter 3. The book, if you haven't read it, is a brilliant history of human attempts to deal with the problem of extreme complexity in aviation, medicine, and other professions. It provides state-of-the-art information about the use of well-designed checklists, especially in Gawande's own field of surgery, where patient outcomes are currently being improved around the world through the simple use of checklists to tame complexity.

Salespeople share the need to tame extreme complexity. Brooks and John found that when the goal is to build a relationship the best discovery sequence is from least intrusive question to most intrusive question. It's true in sales, too. The best structured process for "crystalizing dissatisfaction" adheres to this sequence. Moving from that which is intellectual and safe to that which is personal and emotional (and which makes one vulnerable), requires that we preserve the buyer's self-esteem as we gently cause them to trip over the truth.

Challenging that lacks finesse will be perceived as presuming or even attacking and will shut down a conversation because it damages the buyer's self-esteem. And it's no fun to be around. Remember the know-it-all in your high school class? Picture that person. Did you hang out with him?

We'll come back to an ideal need diagnostic sequence in a moment. Before we do, though, let's finish (at last) the four elements of good questioning suggested by Brooks and John. The final item is tone.

Tone signifies HOW we say WHAT we say. In the Sales Star Model (Chapter 10) tone is referred to as your vocal persona, which along with your personal presence and interpersonal communication skills makes up your style. In sales, style matters more than substance. (I know that's controversial; I'll elaborate when we discuss the style section in the Sales Star Model.)

In sales game film I hear tone that undermines the conversation in the form of:

Nervousness. If we do not purposely choose our vocal persona and personal presence before a sales conversation, just as an actor does before walking onstage, then we will unconsciously broadcast our current emotional state.

Inappropriate joy. Believe it or not, based on thousands of hours of sales game film, salespeople act happy in the face of a buyer's pain. We know our goal is to uncover a problem, and we are happy when we have done so. Better to display practiced indifference (as they call it at Black Duck) or empathy at this juncture. Not drooling fangs.

Accusation. A common failing of today's unverified sales approaches is the use of accusatory language and an accusatory tone. Just yesterday I reviewed a conversation in which the seller asked, "How long have you failed to … ?"

Words like issue, challenge, pain, problem, fail, etc. are all accusatory. They are also unnecessary and have no place in a proper diagnostic conversation. An accusatory tone ensures you will alienate, not persuade. Sadly, there are current, popular sales training programs that promote this accusatory, pain-only approach to selling.

Enthusiasm. Enthusiasm is contagious. It makes one sick.

Vulnerability. While I'm not sure it fits with Brooks and Johns' findings, and I'm not sure Gong's machine learning can pick up this sort of human nuance, I will add one more key concept. This is 5,000-year-old wisdom, rarely practiced even though it is available: Not only do we need to ask the questions in ascending level of intrusiveness, but as we ask another person to be vulnerable, it is essential that we provide emotional leadership and *display vulnerability first.*

No one wants to say "I love you" first. This is a vital interpersonal communications skill. As I coach people using sales game film, this is the sort of nuance that differentiates top sales performers from others. Since it's not obvious, few figure it out.

But once it is pointed out, almost anyone can do it. It is worth repeating: If you want a buyer to be vulnerable, you must be vulnerable first.

Being smart feels good. But you are not on a sales call to get your personal emotional needs met. If challenging or probing for pain is harsh, threatening, or accusatory, it causes buyers in the real world to shut down. You may have been taught to challenge, but be ever so careful that you are not doing more harm than good. Do as Abraham did when negotiating to save his nephew Lot and his family before God destroyed Sodom. Be a bit confused and vulnerable.

And remember, tone is especially important when employing anti-suggestions; they can be very powerful with the right tone and very dangerous with the wrong tone.

How buyer's buy (from a scientific point of view)

Let's segue from discussing need diagnosis to considering for a moment how buyer's buy. This should allow us to finalize the exact type and sequence of questions that actually work in the real world.

Gestalt theory comes from the discipline of psychology. Thankfully we are no longer reliant solely on psychological theories; we also have access to the physiological science of the brain.

Neuroscientists now understand that the emotional and rational parts and functions of the human brain are more closely intertwined than was previously thought. Sales processes and psychologists anticipated this physiology decades ago. Now we can literally see the interactions with magnetic resonance imaging (MRI).

Dr. Dean Shibata, Assistant Professor of Radiology at the University of Washington, uses brain scans to study how people make decisions. His work allows us to quite literally see how buyers decide.

Shibata scanned the brains of volunteers using a relatively new technique called functional magnetic resonance imaging (fMRI) that allows us to watch the human brain in action, in real-time.

People making personal decisions showed more activity in the ventromedial frontal lobe, a part of the prefrontal cortex in the mammalian brain. This part of the brain is implicated in the processing of risk and fear. It also plays a role in decision making. They didn't use that same part of the brain when they were thinking about impersonal decisions, such as comparing the financial cost of two events.

Intellectual arguments will not cause people to change their behavior.

"Research supports the idea that every time you have to make choices in your personal life, you need to 'feel' the projected emotional outcome of each choice. That feeling guides you and gives you a motivation to make the best choice, often in a split second," says Dr. Shibata.

Shibata is not alone in this view, and says he was inspired by the work of neurologist Antonio Damasio, who has worked with patients who've suffered brain damage. Evidence suggests that when someone suffers an injury to the part of the brain that governs emotion, they may retain normal memory and be able to solve abstract problems, but they will often have trouble making routine, rational decisions such as when to make a doctor's appointment. They seem to get caught in "infinite loops" where they are unable to prune through the various options and decide.

Buyers' decisions in b2b sales

You might ask, "What does this have to do with buyers? They are not making a personal decision in enterprise sales." But the fact is they are. They are deciding to take on the risk of acting as a change agent. And that risk is real.

In consumer sales, the risk is lower. If you buy a new TV and it doesn't work out, it is certainly irritating and a bit of a bother, but rarely earth shattering.

In b2b sales, the risk is higher. If you champion a project at work, and it doesn't work, it might be a career-damaging decision.

Public failure and damage to our career are things we fear deeply.

Back to the need diagnostic

Now might be a good time to bring up an important general principle: People have needs, but they don't want to be vulnerable, so they hide their needs, even from those who can help. It's part of the reason that the default buying process is, as I mentioned earlier, a perfect storm of dysfunction.

Perhaps you'll recall Heidi Grant's excellent description of the phenomenon (see page 52-53), in which she reminds us that very few people enjoy asking for assistance because it's uncomfortable, but also that it's well-nigh impossible for folk to get by without any help.

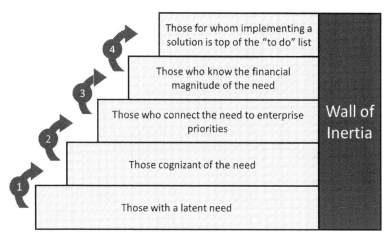

Again, the natural buyer avoids or rushes diagnosis and moves to solutions too quickly. In order to complete a sale we will likely need to slow the process down in order to surface and properly diagnose the need, while at the same time taking steps to protect the buyer's self-esteem.

Four levels of need diagnostic questions

Now let's put all of these broad and disparate thoughts on need diagnosis together into a neat and simple package. There are four sets of need diagnostic questions that can help you overcome what I call the wall of inertia in b2b selling. The wall of inertia is the human desire to be stable, at rest.

The four sets of questions that will allow you to scale (or even breach) the wall of inertia are:

1. Questions to create cognizance help the buyer move from latent need to awareness.
2. Questions to connect the need to organizational priorities help the buyer position his project to win over competing projects.
3. Questions to quantify the financial magnitude of the need help the buyer build the business case.
4. Questions to understand the priority of implementing the solution, so both the seller and the buyer can make a good decision about investing time and resources.

Questions to create cognizance

Questions to create cognizance start with role-specific diagnostic questions. Here are two examples:

- A salesperson who is prospecting might say, *"When I speak to (title/vertical), your colleagues sometimes say (state a need), but I don't know you. Is your perspective different?"* This is a role-specific diagnostic probe which can be used when the buyer has not previously expressed interest. Note it is a message tuned to a specific title and vertical market, it is focused on language of the problem set not the solution set, and it is an anti-suggestion.

- *"Starting off, would you mind sharing a quick overview of what you are looking to accomplish with a new BI solution?"* This is an open diagnostic probe, used if the buyer has already expressed interest by responding to something like a webinar invitation, or by downloading a whitepaper, or by calling in.

Create a safe space to let the need blossom with very open questions, like the one I suggested earlier as a soft entry into the diagnostic: *"You don't really know me and cyber security is a sensitive area.*

Without going too far, is there additional insight you think I should understand?"

Move from the abstract to the specific with a question like: *"Is there a recent instance that stands out in your mind?"*

Understand the history of this need with questions like:

- *"Have there been past efforts to achieve this?"*
- *"Did you make significant progress?"*

Questions to connect the need to enterprise priorities

"Stepping back to the big picture, is the impact on your organization important or relatively insignificant?"

Questions to quantify the financial magnitude of the need

"I don't have much insight into your system economics. Perhaps you can help me understand. You have not mentioned cost. Have you concluded there's no financial impact associated with this?"

NOTE: This is the most difficult of all sales diagnostic questions. The seller must express vulnerability. It must be an anti-suggestion.

Questions to understand the priority of the need to this person

"You are a busy person. My sense is that this may not be on your front burner?"

In the end, the buyer has to convince you that this need is a personal, emotional priority. If they don't, then you will waste your time and theirs. If it is not a personal, emotional priory they will never act. People decide emotionally and justify intellectually.

A quick review

So far in the perfect discovery call we have:

- Created a context for mutual honesty with the mutual agenda, and

- Advanced our (and the buyer's) understanding of the unique need of this buyer, its impact, the business case, and its proper priority with a need diagnostic.

Now it is time to co-create the buyer's utopian vison of the future.

Uncovering the buyer's utopian vision

Still bridling our desire to be smart and solve problems (rather than offering our solution or shoving it down the buyer's throat), we choose the more effective path. We ask the buyer to toss our solution out the window for a moment and describe their utopian vision of the solution. On the heels of a good need diagnostic, buyers in the real word respond with engaged answers. Since people do not argue with their own ideas, this makes selling easy.

Buyer's Utopian Vision				
☐ Customer's baby				
☐ Unique fit				
☐ Deal with no fit				

The Perfect Discovery Call Checklist has three criteria as the quality standard for co-creating the solution vision.

The first is that the buyer describes the solution and it's their baby.

The second is that the solution is a unique fit. If you developed need in an area of your unique strength, this occurs naturally. If the buyer did not mention an important aspect, you can co-create the solution by mentioning the piece they left out. But do not try to talk them into it. It's better to try to talk them out of it. *"John, you did not mention security. Is that because, for this application, it is not really needed?"*

The third is that you must deal with "no fit" situations. If the buyer mentions something you don't do or don't do well, you need to point it out. Oddly, if sellers say, "We can do A, B, and C, but D is not in our wheelhouse. Is that a deal killer?" it helps advance the sale. It might result in you disqualifying them based on lack of fit, which is a good outcome. More often the buyer says, "D is not that important and if you can do A, B, and C, that's awesome!"

Please note this bit of real magic: When you say you can't do D, it convinces the buyer you can do A, B, and C more than any presentation will ever do. A disarming level of honesty is a rare breath of fresh air and a powerful selling stance.

Once we have:

- Created a context for mutual honesty with the mutual agenda,
- Advanced our (and the buyer's) understanding of the unique need of this buyer, it's impact, the business case, and its proper priority with a need diagnostic, and
- Co-created the buyer's utopian vision of the future with our solution,
- It is now the Goldilocks moment to deal with money—not too early and not too late.

Uncover the budget

Dealing with Money			
☐ Explain Pricing Model			
☐ Solid number on table			
☐ With confidence			
☐ "No drip" mobile defense			

BANT might be bunk

BANT is a well-worn sales qualification methodology. The acronym stands for Budget, Authority, Needs, and Timeline. If a prospect can meet those qualifications to your satisfaction, the sale is worth pursuing—or so goes the accepted wisdom.

A Zen *koan* is a riddle that Buddhist monks use to open their minds. Here's a sales *koan* to ponder: The B in BANT is irrelevant.

Most traditional consultative selling methodologies qualify based on the buyer's budget. They implore salespeople to ask, "Do you have a budget set aside for this project?" It stands to reason. After all, we do not want to put tons of time into an opportunity only to find out there's no money, honey.

How to trash rapport – Imagine a poker game in which one of the players asks another, "Can I see your cards for a quick second?"

This question almost never gets the desired response. It's one of way too many sales techniques that have been passed down as gospel in most sales training engagements for decades. Like many of these sacred cows, it collapses under scrutiny. It just flat doesn't work. It blows up in the face of salespeople who dutifully do what someone told them to do. If you are committed to it, remember that people in developing countries are committed to not using latrines based on 20,000 years of habit. That makes it a well-accepted idea; not a good idea.

At least test it. "Take a bold risk. Measure honestly." This is on the wall of another of my favorite clients, Tenable Security. In 2018, their IPO was up 40% on the first day.

In the real world when sellers ask buyers about their budget, it undercuts trust and creates resistance, just as if you asked to see someone's poker hand.

Budget does not matter – The buyer's willingness to make the investment is all that matters.

- A buyer that has the budget and is *not* willing, will not buy.
- A buyer that doesn't have the budget but *is* willing, will find the money to buy.

A buyer's willingness is driven by the cost of the status quo. We'll consider this point in a bit more detail in the section on opportunity planning in the next chapter.

How to talk about money

As much as I value questions in a consultative sales process, this is a good place to make a statement.

Put the price on the table with confidence and conviction. Seriously. I suggest the seller just put the price on the table with confidence and conviction. If everything to this point has been done well, a careful buyer may still flinch.

The typical salesperson responds to the flinch in a pleading voice with, "Where do we need to be to earn your business?"

If you think of the buyer as squeezing a rag and the salesperson as the rag, what will the buyer do when the salesperson drips like that? They keep squeezing. They keep squeezing until the buyer stops dripping.

Train your salespeople to anticipate the flinch and ask them to prepare three no-drip responses in advance. Then under pressure, they will have a plan to fall back on.

By this point we have:

- Created a context for mutual honesty with the mutual agenda,
- Advanced our (and the buyer's) understanding of the unique need of this buyer, it's impact, the business case, and its proper priority with a need diagnostic,
- Co-created the buyer's utopian vision of the future with our solution, and
- The buyer has convinced us they are willing and able to make the necessary investment in time, money, and other resources.

Now is the time to co-build a mutual action plan with the buyer. Think of it as building a bridge across the chasm in the buyer's journey from analysis to action. I have listened to enough sales game film to know that even the largest, and most sophisticated global organizations, do not know how they are

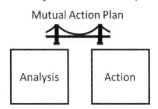

Mutual Action Plan

Analysis	Action

going to decide until they decide. So, co-build the bridge over the chasm with them. Then cross the bridge together with them.

Old school versus selling today

As I've already said, most sales training—even today—includes some form of "closing." It sounds like, "If I can show you a way...."

We cannot ignore the fact that the intention behind an action determines its effect. And "closing" violates the Law of Paradoxical Intent, which (once again) states:

If you're desperate to make something happen, and you attempt to control people and events, you will repel the people who you are trying to persuade and prevent the outcomes you desire.

In fact, attempts at closing will often ensure you do not get a second meeting in opportunities that require many meetings with many people over time.

A modern buying organization has safeguards that prevent an environment where pressure tactics can be used. They require that the due diligence process include professional buyers who are immune to pressure tactics. By and large, senior executives in sizable organizations are also immune to this sort of bullying. Real world sales cycles include opportunities in which you may never meet with the buyer. In today's world, especially in larger corporations, the buyer has a formal process that must be accommodated.

The mutual action plan (MAP) is an adaptation to accommodate this reality. It involves co-building the due diligence process; it is the outcome of negotiating as opposed to dictating. It allows for a modern buying process that might be done from a distance and might include a formal, competitive process. The MAP anticipates savvy buyers who cannot be bullied.

Since it was built on mutual agreement as opposed to fear of conflict, it does not require you to meet with the buyers in order to close. Since it was not a high-pressure tactic, it does not result in being locked out of the process.

A quick history

In the 1980s it was my old Army habit to write after-action reports; I adapted the habit to sales calls. One day, as I was typing up my notes, I decided it might make sense to email them to the buyer to help him remember, too. Since I had already done the work of typing, why not?

Once sharing my notes with the buyer became habitual, I noticed that my calls improved. My new habit forced me to inspect my process and validate the agreements reached with the buyer. That bears repeating. Writing a recap completes the cybernetic loop and accelerates your learning curve. That is why leaders in the Army write after-action reports. It is why Air Force pilots conduct a rank-less debriefing after an operation, using black box recordings of the flight to ensure accuracy. This review step accelerates the learning curve of war fighters. It's why professional and college sports coaches use game film. They all close the cybernetic loop to advance the skills of the teams.

Furthermore, I found that sometimes people would push back on what I wrote in my recap. And I was grateful for it. It proved the old adage that the great enemy of communication is the illusion of it. Until it is in writing, you can't really be sure what was agreed to.

I also noticed that prospects who pushed back almost always became customers. Someone who takes co-building the MAP that seriously is committed.

Over time I naturally turned the use of a written recap into an experiment. 80% of the deals done with a written MAP closed. Only 20% of those without one closed. I do of course realize that these numbers are pretty convenient, and would not blame you for suspecting that I'm just (poorly and transparently) applying the Pareto principle here. I assure you I'm not. You can do a split test and confirm the numbers for yourself. And I encourage you to do so.

The written MAP also solved a big sales management problem, a problem that companies spend millions to solve with CRM: It made the forecast more accurate.

I have no idea how to get to 100%, but 80% is achievable at an organizational level. Importantly, it is 80% across the board; not 12% for one rep, 49% for another, and 90% for your top salesperson.

The reason it works is that you are measuring customer activity, not sales activity.

Since my partner GuruGanesha Khalsa and I first introduced this concept as the Ultimate Contract in the Sandler High-Tech Selling System it has become widely accepted. The MAP has been called a number of things: Next Step Letter, Ultimate Contract, Close Plan, Mutual Outcome Plan. It has also been misused and corrupted along the way.

Buyers love a mutual action plan, if it is properly done.

I've been privileged to work with the Salesforce sales team. Here's an email one of their salespeople shared with me in 2017 when she first used a MAP.

> *Kristy,*
> *I am very impressed with your systematic approach to sales, how you listen, only address what matters to the prospect, convey in a clear manner the expectations, money and the clear next steps. I am not young, so I have seen a lot, and it's rare to meet someone who knows how to do what you do and use the approach you are using. Where did you learn this?*
> *Linda*

MAPs and intent

Kristy was successful because of her intent. A MAP driven by the intent to ensure clarity of communication is applauded by a buyer. A MAP driven by the desire to hold the buyer accountable will be rejected by the buyer.

Wall Street puts pressure on CEOs, who then pass that pressure on to sales leadership, who dutifully pass it along to the sales team, who then most unwisely pass it on to customers. If this is how the MAP is used it will fail because customers really hate pressure.

In addition, the forecast reverts to being less accurate under pressure. As pressure increases, so does lying. As I write this, a sales rep I know very well told me about a deal she knows will not close by the end of the quarter (next week), yet her boss's boss has reported it as Closed/Won. He did that under pressure. It was self-preservation.

The company she works for—where lying seems to be inadvertently (and counterproductively) encouraged—calls the MAP a Close Plan. They have lost their way and corrupted the process. It is not serving the interests of the buyer or the seller. It is not truly mutual. Stuff flows downhill in all organizations. The bigger a company gets, the higher the hill, the greater the volume and velocity of the stuff, and the deeper the pile at the bottom. You salespeople are not at the bottom. Your customers are.

As CEO, you can fall into this trap so terribly easily. I honestly thought the private purchase of public companies by private equity firms would help with this. Unfortunately, it just gets worse. Cherish the time you have as an entrepreneur prior to funding and IPOs. When guys with spreadsheets are in charge—and I do love the VC—sales leadership savvy can easily go out the window.

There is something to Salesforce CEO Marc Benioff's spirit of aloha. Salesforce offices feature meditation rooms. I know many scoff at that kind of crunchy California behavior. But Kristy got this compliment because she used a sales technique (MAP) with the right intent (to ensure clear communication). Her intent is to achieve clarification and not enforcement. Buyers love to be understood. They do not like to be controlled. Take a lesson from Salesforce's aloha spirit. Go meditate! Then relax. Then call a customer.

To master sales techniques, you have to embrace the philosophy behind the techniques.

When the question "Will you take this man to be your husband?" is asked at the altar, the groom is not wondering what the bride is about to say. Usually. Hopefully.

Since buyers are willing participants in co-creating the MAP, I suggest that modern sellers stop using the word "close," which is something you do to someone. And to doors. I suggest modern, sophisticated buyers will reject "closers." I suggest "co-building" a decision process that the buyer and seller co-create and co-commit to executing. I further suggest that, while it may feel like a loss of control to collaborate instead of dictate, the seller actually gains much greater control because the buyer is a willing participant. Do it WITH them rather than TO them.

Mechanics of a mutual action plan

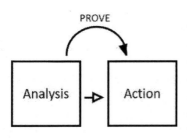

The mutual action plan is a step-by-step process to which both parties are mutually committed that leads to the ultimate "yes" or "no" in a timeframe with which both are comfortable. The specific form of each question determines how well it will work.

Mutual Action Plan				
☐ When is the latest?				
☐ Past, similar process?				
☐ No one else cares?				
☐ Co-built				
☐ Clear steps defined				
☐ Let them know you will send it in writing for review				

The sequence of the questions also makes a difference, and of course follows the order recommended by our Harvard PhDs as optimal for building relationships: Least intrusive to most intrusive questions, as follows.

- *When is the latest you would like to see the solution up and running?*

This question establishes the buyer's timeframe. Based in their sense of urgency, we can do a backward planning sequence to drive the timing of every step in the sales cycle. It is worth repeating, the timeline is based on the buyer's sense of urgency and only their sense of urgency. You cannot hasten the ripening of the fruit. Vine-ripened tomatoes are the only good tomatoes.

- *Have you been through a similar process in the past?*

When we ask about a past process, we get a more accurate and detailed understanding of what this process will look like. People remember the good and the bad when asked about the past. When thinking of the future, they tend to be overly optimistic. This means your forecast is overly optimistic.

- *Is it possible you will need the support of others who do not share your desire to get this done?*

One of the worst sales questions of all time is, "Are you the decision maker?" I've heard it too many times on game film and it's never pretty. It forces them to become gatekeepers. They usually say something like, "My boss signs, but she does whatever I recommend." Odd as the phrasing I suggest may seem, in the real world it gets much more truthful and accurate answers to this very sensitive and intrusive question.

- *What are the steps we will need to go through to get to a point where you can make a comfortable, informed decision on whether or not to pull the trigger?*

This is not an abstract conversation. You are both opening your calendars and creating a plan. It's not unusual for a buyer to name one or two steps and stop. You may need to ask them if that gets them to a point where they will be comfortable deciding, or if there will be additional steps. Keep going until the MAP leads all the way to the ultimate yes or no. If you can't co-create a MAP that leads to the end of the sales cycle, then there is no end.

Finally, I suggest you let them know you will recap the conversation in an email to ensure that you understood everything. Then send them a written MAP (to download a sample MAP, please go to www.softwaresalesgurus.com, click the "Sales Tips" tab, then the "Coaching Toolbox" tab and use the password "goodselling").

If you can honestly check the boxes below, you have a truly mutual action plan.

- ☐ Is the MAP co-built?
- ☐ Are clear steps to the ultimate yes or no defined?
- ☐ Did the customer confirm a written MAP like the sample on the next page?

Sample MAP	
Subject Line	Recap of our conversation as promised
Opening	Dear Phil, I enjoyed our conversation. Below is the summary of my notes which I promised to send for your review. We covered a lot of ground, so please let me know if I misinterpreted anything we discussed.
Unique Need	**Your needs are:** *(In this section you should write a synopsis of the need in their words. This should be the longest paragraph of the note.)*
Unique Vison	**Your ideal solution would include:** *(A brief, conceptual overview of the solution you co-created with the buyer).*
Money	We discussed an investment of $_____.
Go/No Go Roadmap	**You want a solution in place no later than (date).** To meet your timeframe, we decided on the following plan: (This section is a series of scheduled milestones that lead to the ultimate Yes or No.) Step 1 Step 2 Step 3
Close	Did I get anything wrong? Sincerely, Steve Kraner

Summary of MAP benefits to both buyers and sellers

- The MAP builds customer validation into the sales process.

  The traditional method for measuring the quality of opportunities in the pipeline and the accuracy of the sales forecast is to ask the salespeople to put information into a CRM system. They do, but they do just enough to fill the boxes and keep their boss happy. It creates a garbage in, garbage out forecast.

  In contrast, the MAP is co-built with the buyer and the written MAP is shared with the customer and verified by them, removing the opportunity for salespeople to misunderstand or misreport the real status of an opportunity. If they must co-build the process and verify it with the customer, it ensures the agreement is mutual and real. It makes the forecast accurate. Sometimes customers point out items in the MAP with which they do not agree. As a result, the communication is corrected, and this often saves the opportunity. Subjectivity is removed by verifying the conversations with the customer. The opportunity review becomes an integral part of the sales cycle.

- Because the MAP is written and customer-verified, it can be integrated into the forecast. This ties the sales process to policy and hardwires the sales process into the nervous system of the organization.

- A MAP provides a written record and continuity in a long sales cycle, for both sides. Since it is generally written for the larger, more complex opportunities, with long sales cycles, it helps the seller and the buyer recall where they are in an extended sales cycle.

- Buyers will tell you they love it, if it is properly done. Properly means the intent is to achieve clarification and not enforcement. Just as when a woman dances with a man who leads well, it makes her look good.

- A MAP provides a basis for resource allocation in sales cycles that entail extensive costs of sales. If you know it costs you $100,000 to pursue an opportunity and if you haven't gained agreement on all the steps to the ultimate yes or no, you can decide not to spend the money until you do.

- A MAP ensures that all interested parties in an enterprise sale are on the same page, working with the same information. This is especially important in sales cycles that require a cross-functional, multi-person sales team and a complementary team on the buyer side. The document helps get and keep everyone on both sides informed. And if players change on either side, the document brings new players up-to-speed.

- A MAP is a window into the skill set of the salesperson who negotiated and wrote it. It is a recap of the key elements of qualification. This enables meaningful coaching.

- A MAP completes the feedback loop for salespeople, who can then self-correct. It is a behavior trap, like having a workout partner. Since the MAP requires that you address all the key elements of qualification, you cannot write it unless you asked and got answers to all the hard questions.

If (or better yet, when) you complete all of the above, you've completed the perfect discovery call.

The benefit of an early no

NO is a logical outcome of the perfect discovery call, and a good outcome. Salespeople and their leaders must fully embrace that liberating idea. Chris Boyd of Black Duck Software, in a recent sales mastery session, shared a success that resulted from going for NO. He conducted a discovery call in which he properly disqualified the buyer, who then was so impressed with Chris's disarming honesty that he referred him to someone else in his organization who had the problem

Chris can fix.

In that same mastery session, Gill Libro, a Synopsys sales rep, reported that had disqualified a client for the Synopsys code management solution originally under consideration and in the process generated genuine interest in the Black Duck solution. If you and your team are not getting to graceful NO's, then you will be missing out on the frequent positive outcomes NO creates.

Mastering the perfect discovery call

It's a lot to manage in one hour. No one can do it in one call initially. It may take multiple calls. If there are multiple decision-makers it is best done as a series of individual, one-on-one conversations to allow an optimum environment for diagnosis.

Mastery of this simple, one-page checklist generally takes a person from six to twelve months. Some can never do it.

The sales mastery phase is a period of intensive habit reformation and sales skill building. Sales mastery is attained through the same processes used in sports: Systems, coaching, playbooks, intensive practice, and the use of game film. My recommended cadence is a series of weekly sales mastery sessions, using sales call recordings like game film to coach.

Each salesperson should focus on one of the steps in your own customized sales methodology at a time. Once they demonstrate mastery in a live selling situation, they should move on to the next step. Salespeople and managers will progress at their own pace. The stronger salespeople will succeed more quickly and their example will pull the rest of the team along.

6 SELLING SYSTEM ESSENTIALS, PART 2: THE STRATEGIC SALES PLAYBOOK

As I said before, strategic selling means doing the right things, with the right people, at the right time. It covers the planning of (and afterwards reviewing) the execution of sales. It looks at the big picture. It's the game plan; the overall approach to sales. It's the strategy.

Strategic selling focuses on three primary segments of the sales function: Opportunity management, account management, and territory management. The strategic sales landscape looks something like this:

Some general notes on strategic planning

Great salespeople have a bias to act. They tend to be less interested in planning, which they seem to regard as by its nature dry, cerebral, and to be avoided. Planning is just not natural. Most plans therefore are produced more in the spirit of CYA than because the salesperson believes it's important.

I suggest that planning is critical to operational excellence, and that the best teams make themselves do it, just like the best athletes make themselves work out even when they don't feel like it.

Let's start with a simple question: Why plan?

(Here's a little exercise for you: Take 60 seconds and in the margins list as many reasons as you can for how doing a bit of research, planning, and mapping of an account could be useful. And you're welcome for the small margins!)

There are a number of benefits I always experience, and am always grateful for, which result from it. The discipline of planning:

Crystallizes thinking – 80% of the value is not the plan you produce; it's the thought process you go through to produce it.

Compels action – It's an old engineering principle that once you've formulated the right question, you're more than half way to the answer. That is, once you have the right question, and all the information in one organized place, the right action becomes apparent.

Reduces vulnerability – It keeps you from being blind-sided and helps you think several moves ahead of your competition.

Empowers your team – A major goal of planning is an effective and repeatable process for a collaborative selling effort. Planning enables team selling with direction and information. If we include all the people who touch the account in the planning stage, we multiply our strength beyond the thoughts and capabilities of any one individual.

Facilitates control of multiple accounts – I always think of Ed Sullivan and the guy with the plates. Maybe it's me, but I can't juggle a lot of projects unless I have a file, and records. A regularly updated plan lets me know where I am and what is meant to happen next, at any given moment. So I can pick it up and be back on track in a few seconds.

Promotes intelligent resource allocation – Fire, ready, aim is bad strategy. You cannot do everything for everybody. If you don't consciously allocate your time, the squeaky wheel will always get the grease. The best customers often get taken a bit for granted.

Highlights relationship vs. transaction – When you move into an account manager role, you do of course need to produce transactions, but you also need to add a level of attention and concern for the relationship beyond the transaction. You must balance short-term pursuit of opportunities with a long-range investment in the relationship. For example, you may set up a meeting between one of your executives and a client executive even though there's no current sales opportunity involved. It's very easy to give your full attention to the short-term transaction; planning keeps you thinking and acting for the long-term too.

Levels of sales planning

Here's a high level overview of sales planning functions and responsibilities:

CEO: Business plan

Senior sales leader: Sales and marketing plan

Sales team:

- Opportunity – Major opportunities require a strategic selling process: Plan, execute, review
- Account – Strike a balance between advancing a transaction and developing the relationship
- Territory – Focused on triage; in other words, segregates

customers to allow for the best return for the invested sales effort

- Call plan – Produced for each specific sales call

Opportunity Management

Major opportunities are typically engaged on three fronts, which must be understood from the buyer's frame of reference. That is to say, in planning a sales campaign for a large opportunity, three discrete centers of gravity must be considered and attended to:

1. Technology – WHAT do we (the buyers) need?
2. Financial – HOW MUCH financial return vs. competing projects?
3. Political – WHO do we trust?

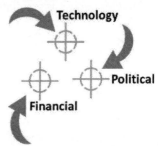

We shall look more carefully at these centers of gravity shortly, but first let's take a look at the sales factors that make opportunity planning useful and relevant.

What makes a complex deal complex?

Multiple decision makers – Selling to groups and committees made up of people with conflicting goals requires disciplined thought and careful planning prior to action. Navigating the political landscape becomes a critical component of the sale.

Financial evaluation – There is always internal capital competition and the larger projects will be subjected to a more rigorous financial analysis.

Senior level approval – Large investments require executive approval.

Multiple players on your cross-functional selling team – Many salespeople are outstanding individual contributors, but have never learned to effectively lead a collaborative team selling effort. Leading a team sales effort requires a particular set of skills that can (fortunately) and must be learned in order to successfully manage major sales opportunities.

Formal buying process – Large projects are rarely undertaken on the whim of an individual in the hyper-competitive modern marketplace. Customers now invariably use a formal buying process for large purchases.

Longer sales cycle – Like mammals, the bigger they are, the longer the gestation period. Controlling the long sales cycle requires a high degree of structure and documentation.

Increased competition – Buyers also strive to create a competitive environment.

Large investment in resources – Both the buyer and the seller can spend hundreds of thousands of dollars in the evaluation process.

Increased sales pressure – The pursuit of a major opportunity often creates a large binary on the salesperson's forecast. If they win they overachieve. If they lose they fail.

How a strategic sales process helps in the opportunity assessment and development environment

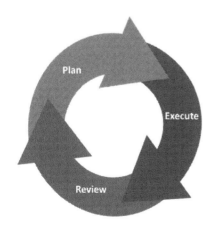

A strategic sales process provides a cogent, repeatable, and effective process for:

- Assessing opportunities – making good bid/no bid decisions
- Planning – establishing the purpose prior to acting
- Executive access and influence
- Influencing selection criteria

- Understanding the political layer and how to sell to groups and committees
- Building the financial case
- Mobilizing the cross-function sales team

Major Opportunity Pursuit Plan

Below is my unexpurgated template for developing and executing a competitive sales strategy for a major opportunity (to download the Major Opportunity Pursuit Plan, please go to www.softwaresalesgurus.com, click the "Sales Tips" tab, then the "Coaching Toolbox" tab and use the password "goodselling"). It is comprehensive. You cannot be too prepared for contingencies. The generals (and coaches) are right to remember that planning is everything even though plans are nothing. Because while it is true that most plans fall apart when the first shot is fired (or the defense blitzes), it is also true that the process of planning prepares you for every imaginable eventuality.

Here are all the things that should always be included in your sales opportunity deliberations:

MAJOR OPPORTUNITY PURSUIT PLAN
ACCOUNT NAME:
OPPORTUNITY NAME:
DATE PREPARED:
PREPARED BY: *While the sales lead will prepare this document, it should not be done in a vacuum. Involve everyone who touches the customer, those who should be connected with this customer, and the customer.*

INDUSTRY BACKGROUNDER:
A brief overview of the customer's industry: The major players and overall environment (economic, regulatory, technology, and major trends). Focus on the things that most impact the customer and are therefore top of mind for executives.

ACCOUNT BACKGROUNDER:
A brief overview of the company, their business or lines of business, financial performance, leadership, history, recent changes, challenges, executive vision, and major initiatives.

CUSTOMER ORGANIZATION:
Provide an overview of the company leadership, major functional areas, and organization.
- *Have there been recent changes in leadership? Why?*
- *Have there been recent changes in the org chart? Why?*

Psychographics:
- *Do they use outside help or do most things in-house?*
- *Are they open to value or price-focused?*
- *Do they view vendors and service providers as partners or is their approach adversarial?*
- *Early adopters or conservative?*

OUR RELATIONSHIP WITH THIS CUSTOMER:
Provide a brief history of our relationship with this customer.
- *Where do we have relationships?*
- *Where do we wish we had relationships?*

PROJECT REQUIREMENTS:
- *What is the business driver – need or aspiration?*
- *Does the problem have executive visibility?*
- *What is the most senior level at which the need is recognized?*
- *What is the customer's Utopian vision of a solution?*
- *What are the timeframes?*

BID/NO-BID CONSIDERATIONS:
- *If we win is it good business?*
- *Is this the best current target?*

CUSTOMER EVALUATION PROCESS:
- *How will they decide and when?*
- *What are the selection criteria?*
- *Did we influence the selection criteria?*
- *Do the selection criteria favor us?*

OUR SOLUTION:
- *Describe our solution.*
- *How does our solution address the need?*
- *Are there aspects of the need we don't address?*
- *How does our solution compare to the customer's Utopian vision of the solution?*
- *Is it a unique fit?*

THEME:
- *What is our theme for our proposal?*
- *Is the entire cross-functional team aware of and reinforcing our theme?*

FINANCIAL CASE:
- *Who is leading the financial analysis on the customer side and how will they analyze the financial case?*
- *Are we involved in the financial analysis?*
- *With what other projects is this project competing for funding?*
- *What is the investment required to implement the solution?*
- *Is the customer willing and able to make this investment?*
- *Who owns the budget?*
- *Is it funded?*

COMPETITIVE ASSESSMENT:
List each selection criteria and then assess how our solution fares and how each competitor fares in each area.

SALES STRATEGY SELECTOR (to download the Sales Strategy Selector, please go to www.softwaresalesgurus.com, click the "Sales Tips" tab, then the "Coaching Toolbox" tab and use the password "goodselling"):

1. *The right thing*
   A. *Offensive – Do we have a current advantage?*
      - *Attack piecemeal – Is there a smaller project scope we can break out and win quickly and decisively?*
      - *Frontal attack – Do we have a current, clear and overwhelming advantage?*
      - *Flanking attack – Can we change or expand the scope of the project to improve our competitive position?*
   B. *Defensive – Are we at a current disadvantage?*
      - *No bid?*
      - *Delay and develop.*
   C. *Co-exist – Can we avoid a fight and still win a piece of business?*

2. *The right people*
   - *Have we completed an Opportunity X-Ray?*
   - *Did the members of the cross-functional pursuit team help complete the X-Ray?*
   - *Have the pursuit team members been briefed on the current X-Ray?*
   - *What is our position with the key people?*
   - *What is our plan to improve our current competitive position?*

3. *The right time*
   - *Accelerate?*
   - *Delay?*

> **CROSS-FUNCTIONAL SALES SEAM:**
> *List the members of the cross-functional sales team involved in this opportunity.*
> - *Do we need executive support?*
> - *Is there support we need but do not have?*

CROSS-FUNCTIONAL TEAM ACTION PLAN (to download the Cross-functional Team Action Plan, please go to www.softwaresalesgurus.com, click the "Sales Tips" tab, then the "Coaching Toolbox" tab and use the password "goodselling"):
Action
- *When scheduled?*
- *When completed?*
- *Who on our team?*
- *Who on their team?*

Opportunity management centers of gravity

As I mentioned, complex sales require planning at the opportunity level. And planning at the opportunity level must usually take into account three centers of gravity: Political, financial, and technology.

Technology – The first (and most obvious) focal point in selling to a large enterprise is the identification of the need, the problem, or the aspiration. What does the prospective buyer want or need, and can your solution provide it?

Financial – Business leaders are taught to make decisions by reducing all considerations to one common unit: Dollars.

The cost of status quo has three components:

1. Current cost that can be removed
2. Future cost that can be avoided
3. Opportunity cost (future income that can be generated, but is not today)

While most sellers focus on the size of the buyer's budget versus the buyer's own price, the comparison is a non sequitur. The buyer's willingness to invest is driven by the cost of the status quo.

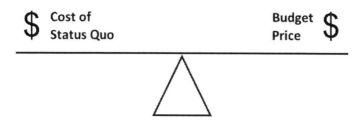

In the mind of the buyer, the price and the budget are one and the same thing in relation to the perceived cost of the status quo. The larger the cost of the status quo, the larger the budget (or price) that is justified in the buyer's mind.

Sellers add value by co-building the business case, not by asking silly sales questions like, "Sir, do you have a budget set aside for this?" If the cost of the status quo isn't a lot bigger than the price, you need to help them see all the unseen costs of leaving well enough alone. Otherwise, the CFO will just say no.

Unfortunately, most technical buyers do not speak the language of the board room. In the real world, many technical buyers are not trained to think in terms of building the business case. They think in terms of technology. They do not think in terms of dollars. So they make technical arguments to financial decision makers. Since they are speaking the wrong language, they often fail to get funds.

And what's more, there is always internal capital competition. There are a lot of technically feasible projects. Everyone wants the CFO to fund their project. Since all companies have finite cash, technically feasible projects will not be funded unless they have a stronger financial argument than competing projects.

Funding usually comes from financial decision makers who ask, "Which of my current investment opportunities will create the greatest, quickest, most certain return on my investment?" In short, the winner is the project that provides the:

- Quickest payback (Your project needs to demonstrate quicker payback than other projects. A CIO told me recently he looks for return the same quarter.)
- Largest payback (Your project has to show a return that is bigger than competing projects.)
- Most tangible and certain payback (The return promised by your project needs to be more credible than the return promised by competing projects.)

If there is nothing on the left side of the seesaw, it isn't going to happen.

<u>Political</u> – When selling into a large enterprise, never underestimate the importance of corporate politics. I was sitting in a staff meeting with a company's president and sales VPs. The conversation revolved around negotiating, discounting, and holding the line on price.

One sales manager said, "If we can prove technical superiority, then I can discount less. But if I can't prove product superiority you can't expect me to hold the line on price!"

And then a deal at Major Media Co. came up. They commented on the fact that it had closed at $1.2M with little discount. I was intrigued.

I later ran into the rep who had closed the Major Media Co. deal and congratulated him. When I asked him about the deal, he said, "It came in at a great price, but I was concerned it wouldn't close because there wasn't really a technical or business problem. We replaced an incumbent solution that worked. The business wasn't really impacted by the change. It was just that Major Media Co. had three new executives who wanted to make their mark and they decided to move away from the incumbent solution."

Politics very often trumps product. The manager who was focused on demonstrating product superiority is apparently not aware that what powerful people want trumps technology. It is not too much to say that value can be defined as "what powerful people personally want."

Because this manager has a fundamental misconception about the basis of value, until he becomes better informed he is doomed to:

- have only "speed and feed" conversations with IT people,
- never have enough sales executives,
- always have long sales cycles,
- need to discount frequently, and perhaps most distressingly,
- train every member of his team to do the same.

He's not focused on the primary factor that determines value in the big deals. Even the rep who closed the deal thought the absence of technical trouble meant there was no value.

Prior to Copernicus's insight, people thought the Earth was the center of the universe. In technology sales, it is natural to think technology is the center of the universe. In both cases, if we operate with a fundamental misconception, outcomes are hard to fathom and the universe seems capricious.

In enterprise selling, the center of the universe is what powerful people personally want. What you *think* justifies the deal is irrelevant. What *does* justify the deal is whatever is emotionally important to the most senior buyer.

The best product does not win. The best salesperson wins.

The Opportunity X-Ray

The Opportunity X-Ray mentioned in the major opportunity plan above is a tool designed to debrief large opportunities. Its intended purpose is to:

- Capture the most critical information about the opportunity in one place. Because several players are involved on both sides in complex sales, it is important that all of the information about the key players on the customer team be captured in one, central location so your whole selling team can see it, contribute to the collective knowledge, and act in unison.

- Gain an accurate and dispassionate view of your competitive position.
- Develop a plan to improve your competitive position.

The Players

1. **Signer:** The final decision-maker.
2. **Financial:** The person who does the financial evaluation of the project.
3. **Project Manager:** The project lead. Most big deals have a person in this role that the *Signer* handpicked.
4. **Legal/Contracts:** The Pitt Bull at the end of the process brought in to negotiate.
5. **User:** Cares about how it will affect their daily lives.
6. **Coach(s):** People who want you to win and will help you.

The Opportunity X-Ray tool (see next page; to download the Opportunity X-Ray tool, please go to www.softwaresalesgurus.com, click the "Sales Tips" tab, then the "Coaching Toolbox" tab and use the password "goodselling")

Opportunity X-Ray

Buying Role	Name Title	Trust		Need	Importance 1-10	Plan to Address
		Sales Team	Company			
Signer						
Financial						
P.M.						
Legal						
User						
Coach						

Account Management

The (former) lone wolf

As I progressed in my sales career, a successful colleague took me aside and told me that when I was pursuing large opportunities or managing key accounts, I could no longer operate as a lone wolf. The secret to her own success, she said, was big deals and teamwork to get them done. That simple. And that difficult. Because she never missed the annual club trip, I took her advice seriously.

At her suggestion, I sought out a service support specialist in my company who had regular after-the-sale contact with my client. She knew more about the customer than I did and had clear ideas about how we could grow the business.

It was then that I realized I should see myself as the leader of a cross-functional sales team. I'd be wise to consult with everyone who touched my customers, put that insight on a page or two, and then share it back with the whole team.

And indeed, when I asked them to help and let them know what was needed, it worked. I went to Maui that year.

Key account leadership responsibility

As a key account manager, you have a leadership responsibility. You are the leader of a cross-functional sales team.

While account plans are OFTEN created ONLY for the sake of compliance, your account planning (as the leader of a team) is a process you can use to:

- Engage and involve everyone who touches the customer— on-site consultants, S.E., customer support, etc.
- Empower every member of the cross-functional team with direction and knowledge.

Key account planning

Split Test

A large global software company did a one-year key account management program for half of their salespeople. The results were rather remarkable: Those who did not have the training sold (on average) $200,000 that fiscal year. Those who learned and incorporated the planning process averaged $700,000.

Rules to live by:

- Designate top tier accounts because you can only efficiently develop plans for about 20% of your accounts.

- Don't do your planning in a vacuum. Involve the customer. Involve everyone on your team who touches the customer. Don't make it up.

- Mobilize all of the company's resources, across all functions and at all levels. Build executive-to-executive relationships between your customer's key leaders and your product management, practice leaders, R&D, and other senior leaders.

Key account plan template

There are many key account management programs with account planning worksheets. The flaw in most of these programs is that they try to create a planning process that will work for everyone. The worksheets end up being so big and cumbersome that no one ever keeps up with them.

The best way to make sure the planning gets done (and is not overkill) is to customize the planning process and documents. Again, make it as light as possible. Below is a basic key account planning process/template to use as a starting point (to download the Key Account Plan tool, please go to www.softwaresalesgurus.com, click the "Sales Tips" tab, then the "Coaching Toolbox" tab and use the password "goodselling").

KEY ACCOUNT PLAN

ACCOUNT:
Name of the key account.

DATE:
Prepare the plan annually and review it with the cross-functional sales team quarterly.

CROSS-FUNCTIONAL SALES TEAM:
List everyone who has contact with the customer.

INDUSTRY/OPERATING ENVIRONMENT OVERVIEW:
Describe the industry, the operating environment, the major players, and trends because these things drive the executive-level thinking of your customer.

ACCOUNT OVERVIEW:
Describe the organization, provide an organizational chart, describe the major divisions, missions, major initiatives and recent or pending organizational changes. Make a note of who you know and who you should know.

GROWTH PLAN:
Remember there are three ways to grow revenue: Get more customers, drive more purchases per customer, and increase the average order size. Two of the three can be most easily accomplished with current customers.

- *Plan to increase orders per customer.*
  NOTE: If you are not selling every customer everything you sell, remember it's not that they aren't buying – they just aren't buying from you.
- *Plan to increase order size.*

ACTIVE OPPORTUNITIES:
Include a current Opportunity X-Ray for each opportunity.

ADDITIONAL RESOURCES NEEDED:
Is there support you need but do not have?

And for good measure, here's the tool I use to keep my cross-functional team working smoothly and effectively:

CROSS-FUNCTIONAL TEAM ACTION PLAN				
1. Sketch out a full-year plan. Do not let the perfect become the enemy of the good. Make progress. 2. Keep this up-to-date and keep your team informed.				
Action	Who on our team	Who on their team	When Scheduled	When Completed

Territory Management

Reasons to designate sales territories

<u>Coverage</u> – Territories focus salespeople on a set of customers, to ensure hunting versus cherry-picking.

<u>Cost of Sales</u> – Territories reduce overlap, so customers and prospects are called on by one person or under the lead of one person.

<u>Customer Service</u> – Assigning responsibility to a single salesperson helps to ensure that all customers and prospects receive the right level of attention and service.

<u>Performance</u> – Properly designed territories allow you to fairly and accurately judge a salesperson's performance, because you can create a reasonable and rational goal, then measure against that goal.

A properly sized territory is not so big and exclusive that a salesperson can succeed by cherry-picking.

Not everyone should designate territories!

Reasons not to set up territories

<u>Small sales team, big market</u> – In this case you *should* cherry-pick the low hanging fruit.

<u>Your sales or delivery teams are specialized</u> – In this case it may make more sense to organize by product or practice than by customer.

<u>Network marketing</u> – I don't mean Amway, but it's pretty much the same concept. If your sales are made on the basis of existing relationships or personal contacts, then you may be better off with no territory structure. An example is a company that sells decision-making software through consultants who specialize in decision making and who can recommend the product.

Suggestions for designating sales territories

<u>Sales Potential</u> – You need more than a dartboard. If the territory has insufficient potential your best salespeople will leave the company for greener (and bigger) pastures. Population or sales history may or may not be a reasonable basis for assigning territories. Often you can find an accurate proxy for sales potential. For sales training, for example, the number of people on a long-established subscription list will give you a very accurate view of what a given territory can do. For software, the installed base of a competitor or some related product might be a good basis.

<u>Physical Size</u> – It's a long way between accounts in New Mexico and not so far in New Jersey. Is a salesperson's time spent traveling or making sales calls? Should some territories be covered by telesales or

other channels?

<u>Adequate Coverage</u> – Is the salesperson able to service all accounts and dedicate enough time to prospecting in the green field space to develop new prospects? Growing organizations often find that they are faced with a need to reduce the size of territories, but the existing sales staff resists the change. I suggest you remind them that there are basically two choices:

1. If you are with a successful and growing company your territory will tend to get smaller and your quota bigger.
2. If you want a growing territory and a shrinking quota you should go work for a dying company.

Here's the template I use to analyze and triage a sales territory and prepare a winning campaign plan.

TERRITORY PLAN
TERRITORY:
PREPARED BY:
DATE PREPARED:

TERRITORY OVERVIEW:
• *Target market description*
• *Geographical description*
• *Current accounts triaged*
    a) *Proactive allocation of a bigger share of time and attention*
    b) *Economy of force*
    c) *Promote or fire*
• *Target accounts triaged*
    a) *Only pursue these*
    b) *Take these if they come to you*
    c) *Avoid*
• *Other key points*

TRIAGE PROCESS EXAMPLE:
Not all customers are equal.

- *What is the profile of an A, B and C customer? (Example: "A" customers value engineering services and buy solutions. "B" customers are transactional and price sensitive, but buy large quantities on a regular basis. "C" customers are small, sporadic and price sensitive.)*
- *Who are the "A" accounts you have identified in the territory? They are the ones who want what you have and have what you want.*
- *Prospecting plan to develop more "A" customers (Example: dedicate engineers along with salespeople in the territories. The engineers spend most of their time with "A" customers because they are goaled on services sales and put time in where their services are valued and will be purchased. These customers buy at the best margins.)*
- *Coverage plan for "B" customers (Example: You value these customers and they are a significant revenue contributor, but they buy at slimmer margins and do not value engineering value add. So the ISR's provide the primary coverage for these customers — responsive, efficient in getting quotes out, and lowest cost of sales.)*
- *Coverage plan for "C" customers (Example: Take an occasional order, but not much time is spent by anyone here. If they become a squeaky wheel, fire or promote to B.)*

ANNUAL TERRITORY GOALS:
What goals have you selected to achieve this year in your territory?

- *Revenue*
- *Strategy (Example: Climb the food chain or value. AM's focus on finding new "A" relationships or promoting "B" to "A" because when they do they have better margins, better account loyalty and are less vulnerable to competitive displacement.)*

PROSPECTING PLAN:

FISCAL YEAR CALENDAR OF EVENTS:

7 SALES FORCE STRUCTURE (AND INFRASTRUCTURE)

Your Sales Team

Sales force structure

As we saw in the first chapter, the sales force structure is determined by the selling process in the same way that the head coach of any successful sports team carefully defines the positions and roles of the players. The behaviors needed to succeed in each role are well-defined, allowing you to select people with the right background.

Remember too that sales is more than just a homogeneous, singular role. There are a lot of different jobs, capabilities, and responsibilities that fall into the category labelled "Sales" in a company and they require different attributes and behaviors to succeed.

Let's take another look at the sales environments we discussed in Chapter 4, and replace them with the types of salespeople that will be required to meet the unique needs of the different environments. The different environments require very different skillsets, different natural talents and abilities, different personalities, perhaps even different DNA.

Sales Types

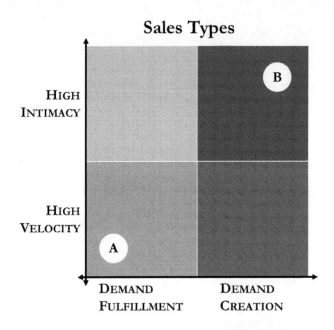

Sales Type A may be at the inbound telesales at Dell or Oracle.

Sales Type B may be an ERP sales rep, dealing with large, complex opportunities with multiple levels of approval.

Can rep A do rep B's job? Most people agree the answer is no.

Can they even be trained to do it? Many people assume you could train rep A to do rep B's job. Experience indicates otherwise. The two jobs seem to require two different sets of DNA.

What would happen if you put a Type B in an A-type job? (I'm well aware of the irony that Sales Type B probably requires a Type A personality, so no snickering.)

Most people assume Rep B is just better, and could easily do Rep A's job. Again, experience indicates this is not true.

Selling is like playing football, as I said. It is a broad term and encompasses a wide variety of jobs and skill sets. If you want someone to make outbound dials to set appointments, you had better hire for that.

From simple to complex

The simplest sales force structure is, of course, the owner who does it all.

The most complex is the multi-tier structure at the largest companies.

Each layer of the segmented sales force requires the right person, with the right training and the right compensation plan. Managers at each layer need the right coaching and management tools and practices.

At most entrepreneurial companies the structure will be fairly simple.

Why an entrepreneurial CEO may need more than one sales role

- Some sales jobs require different skills sets and even different DNA
  - Hunters versus farmers
  - Selling services versus products
  - Commercial versus federal sales
- Some sales jobs must be separated because if one person is responsible for both jobs, they will ignore one.
  - Prospecting is often done by an inside sales team, under close supervision. If left to outside salespeople, they never seem to have time to do it.
  - Maintenance renewal sales is another example. If left to a true hunter, it won't get done.
- Some sales jobs require a different compensation plan than others.
  - You want a high commission for a transactional role.
  - A higher base salary is required for a longer-term focus. Major federal project pursuit requires a seasoned, senior capture manager and requires a relatively high base salary due to the long-term nature of the effort.

An added benefit

A segmented sales force structure provides a career and development path for salespeople.

Junior salespeople may start out in the inside sales "farm team" doing the less desirable work under close supervision. This allows you to attract people to serve in less desirable roles, because they can work their way to a better job. It also allows you to develop talent.

Many sales leaders recognize that their best senior salespeople had prospecting roles early in their careers. Prospecting in a structured inside sales environment is a crucible which produces good discipline, sharp skills, and emotional resilience.

A final practical note for start-ups

One of the most common sales force structure questions we face early is whether we should have one all-encompassing sales role in which each individual salesperson is responsible for prospecting, new business development, and account management, or whether these roles ought to be split up among specialists.

I have two clients who are identical in every way (including the use of my High-Tech Selling System at the system level) except one. The singular difference between them is that one of them requires their salespeople to do everything, while the other set up a call center which does the prospecting and hands off leads to the field sales team.

Both companies are successful. But over time, the differentiator is having a predictable impact. Salespeople at both companies receive an ongoing annuity from their accounts, and the nature of the sales cycle for both companies requires daily prospecting. Once salespeople at the first company (the ones who are required to do everything) began to receive large monthly annuity checks, they began to cool to the tedious discipline of daily prospecting. It turns out there are circumstances in which success can actually demotivate the very behaviors that caused the success.

The company with the all-encompassing sales role eventually hit a plateau; the one with the (closely-supervised) call center did not, and continues to grow.

It typically makes sense to go to three distinct sales roles as soon as it's feasible: sales development reps, field sales, and customer success managers.

Sales force infrastructure

While we could discuss an almost infinite variety of topics in this section, instead we'll focus on just three important elements of sales infrastructure: Lists, customer relationship management (CRM), and call recording

Lists

It's amazing to me how often I find that CEOs allow their sales effort to be list-constrained. The senior leadership of the company must understand:

- Their target market
- Where to find constituents of that market
- Where to buy a list

If you don't know who your target market is and where you can find them, I'd suggest you might not be taking your business seriously enough. I'd also suggest you read Chapter 12 (Strategic Marketing) very carefully indeed. And if you are avoiding buying a list because it's too expensive, I'd urge you to consider the hidden cost of asking your sales team to create a list.

CRM

This can be an efficient way to hardwire the selling system into the nervous system of the organization. Automating your sales efforts can result in:

- Increased efficiency
- Better communication between leadership, marketing, sales, and delivery
- Better customer care
- Improved ability to coach salespeople
- Better accountability

Why CRM fails: Pitfalls to avoid

It's like buying new golf clubs: If that's all you do, it won't improve your game. Salesforce.com actually uses their own tools. They also hire sales trainers (including me) to train their salespeople in a sales methodology.

"One of the big things [Salesforce.com is] struggling with is the attrition issue. The majority happens with the little implementations that have not really bought in, or [after] a corporate standard has been delivered when Salesforce.com is used as a stopgap."
— *Laura Preslan, CRM research director at AMR Research*

Data entry is tedious. Top salespeople do use some sort of contact management and scheduling system. They see the value in scheduling follow-ups, keeping notes, maintaining personal notes on contacts, etc. A top rep told me recently that as he tries to make a simple note on a conversation, he has to go through several buttons that require him to do things like link the note to an opportunity. The conversation may not have been linked to an opportunity, but the system won't save the note unless he responds. He uses a copy of ACT! at home because it's easy to use. The corporate system makes data entry unnecessarily tedious. It's like swimming in a straitjacket.

Sales reps don't benefit from using the system, and don't buy in. This problem usually is the result of systems built by sales management to serve the needs of management (reports, forecasts, activity tracking, etc.) without providing functions that make a rep want to open the laptop and log on (easy access to information and sales tools, leads, accurate information on product availability, etc.).

Salespeople game the system. Some reps sandbag (intentionally understate) the pipeline so they can look like a hero. Some forecast deals that are nowhere near closing to buy a few weeks or months of glory, or survival.

<u>**Monitoring quantity and ignoring quality**</u>. The metrics you track must be measured in terms of both *quantity* (which most SFA/CRM packages do) and *quality* (which they don't). If you measure quantity only, you will probably get more. If you demand more proposals, you will

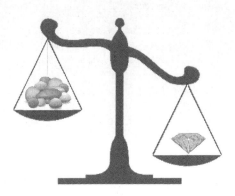

get them. However, the value and quality of the proposals tends to go down, just to satisfy the quantity requirement. Either revenue does not improve, or worse, it is adversely affected as morale drops. As you can see in the picture, one diamond outweighs (is more valuable than) a whole pile of rocks.

In fact, quality versus quantity is typically an inverse relationship: The higher the quantity, the lower the quality, and vice versa. It's a pretty common picture. I might even say it's a truism. We'll look more carefully at the quandary of quality versus in Chapter 10: Coaching Salespeople (Creating Sales Stars).

Another related problem is that you may find it difficult to discern whether your salespeople are really making the calls, or just gaming the system. Are you really getting more, or does it just look that way?

<u>**Asking for too much information.**</u> The solution to increasing sales is not more paperwork. Pick a few key things to track.

No management follow-up. Your salespeople:

1. Do what they get paid to do.
2. Do what their manager makes important to them.

If you pick a few things to track and insist that those few things are done, then doing them will soon become a habit. It's proverbial that "what gets measured gets done," or more prosaically, "they do what you check." It turns out that it's true.

In 1929 Elton Mayo discovered that the simple act of monitoring behavior changed the behavior for the better. Western Electric tried to improve productivity by turning up the lights in a plant. Observers monitored productivity and it went up. Mayo suggested one more experiment at the Hawthorne Plant in New Jersey, but he turned the lights down, not up. Still productivity went up. It was the act of monitoring that increased productivity, not the lighting. Behavioral psychology calls it the Hawthorne Effect

Any behavior you'd like to incent will be improved if you find a way to monitor it.

Call recording (a.k.a. game film)

Serious athletes, from football players to golfers to gymnasts to swimmers, use video recordings to observe and optimize their performance. It's called game film. The sales equivalents of game film is call recordings.

Some form of call recording should be part of every sales infrastructure.

Most modern phone systems allow managers to listen in on phone calls, and to record them. Many conference call solutions offer the same features.

A relatively new breed of cloud-based solutions, such as Gong, are designed to make critiquing calls easier for coaches and managers.

In the mastery phase of deploying a selling system, I hold weekly team meetings to review game film as my primary tool, just like a National Hockey League coach. With game film, there is nowhere to hide. Accountability for the quality of interactions is certain and unavoidable. This approach helps to propagate success from the top of the bell curve of talent to the whole team. Game film can be used to expose, understand, and impact Beliefs as much as it does Ability. It is also the key to coaching Style. We'll discuss Beliefs, Ability, and Style in Chapter 10: Coaching Salespeople (Creating Sales Stars).

Optimize the process, and then automate.

8 HIRING SALESPEOPLE

Your Sales Team

People

Once the sales force structure is determined, and each sales role is defined, we can pick the right people for each role.

"It's a lot easier to hire the right people to begin with than to fix them later." — Bradford D Smart, Ph. D

Street people as salespeople

A marketing executive at a global software company asked me to help with trade show lead follow-up. She said they had just done a big trade show in Mexico City and no one was following up on all the leads she had generated. She had her entire sales team from South America and Mexico fly in and wanted me to train them and supervise the follow-up calls.

As part of it she said, "Why don't you write a script?"

I said, "We don't want to ask them to change their game. That's like asking a pro golfer to change his swing the day of the Masters."

She replied, "You could write a script and pull people off the street and do it."

Do you see the problem here?

She is a wonderful person, but she has no concept of what it takes to be a successful salesperson and has no respect at all for the sales function.

I said, "In that case, perhaps you'd be willing to join us and make some calls, too?"

She declined.

The guy

Entrepreneurial CEO's hire "the guy." The guy used to be the '90's wunderkind; the ex-Oracle, Cisco, IBM, PWC hotshot with a terrific track record. You can't take time to develop talent. You have to hire the right people with the skills you need to get things done in 6-18 months. Time doesn't allow for anything else.

Unfortunately, experience indicates that the vast majority of these hotshots aren't so hot. Here's why…

Can't get appointments: A sales VP said, "You can't get appointments with C-level people if you are with a no-name company!" I asked why he thought that was true. He said, "Because at Oracle I called C-level people and got appointments. Now I call and they won't see me!" (Please stop and think about that. If you agree with him, think some more.)

I was one of those guys: I can't criticize these hotshots too much. I was one of them. I remember laughing at a stock broker who complained about how hard it was to get appointments and how frequently they were cancelled. I remember saying, "I've never been stood up for a meeting. What's her problem?"

A dose of humility: When I hung out my sales consulting shingle in 1993 and went to my basement to make cold calls, my perspective changed. I struggled. At the big company I got appointments nearly 100% of the time. On my own, I faced a steady diet of rejection.

The big company brand had carried me.

I had to learn to sell because I really didn't know how.

Sales "Stars"

If you were in tech sales in the '90s, during the pre-Y2K buying binge, you were in a blizzard of purchase orders so intense that they'd stick to you. That monsoon of spending produced a crop of salespeople who thought success was that easy. They felt like they were stars.

These stars are much like the people in Garrison Keillor's fictional Lake Wobegon, where all the women are strong, all the men are good looking, and all the children are above average.

The next time you are with a group of salespeople who cut their teeth in the 1990s, ask who believes themselves to be an above average salesperson. Chances are everyone in the group will raise their hand, which of course is statistically improbable (if not impossible).

If these stars were at a big name company like Oracle, Cisco, Hyperion, Microsoft, SAP, SUN, KPMG, PWC, HP or IBM they suffered a double dose of overconfidence. The company name carried them more than they know. They never developed the skills that salespeople of other eras developed to survive.

Movin' on up

The '90's stars were successful and moved up to sales management. They say things like, "My people can't get appointments with C-level people because C-level people won't meet with salespeople from no-name companies!"

So they whine and give their entire sales team an excuse. They never stop to think that at some point Oracle was a no-name company and someone had to get to C-level people.

Stars never suspect their own skills are the problem.

I've met thousands of these stars and they simply do not realize how much their company's brand and a rising tide helped them.

Hunting

Stars also think that prospecting is beneath their pay grade. So you end up with a sales team that has no hunters. At an early stage company, the key skill is the ability to open doors without the big name to help. You are operating in an environment where there is no existing market and no demand for what you offer.

If you want a prospector, you'd better hire for that.

Impact of a bad sales hire

In sales, a great hire has a positive effect on the whole organization. A top salesperson raises the bar for everyone on the sales team.

The opposite is also true. The impact of a bad hire isn't just about the individual; a bad hire impacts the whole team. Bad salespeople need a lot of help and drag a lot of people into their losses. And one thing worse than making a bad hire is *keeping* someone who's not making it.

Back to Sales Environments

Now might be a good time to recall our discussion in Chapter 7 about whether Sales Type As can do the job of Sales Type Bs, and vice versa. Take another look at the diagram below to refresh your memory, and then move on with the firm conviction that not all sales jobs are equal and not all salespeople are interchangeable.

Sales Environments

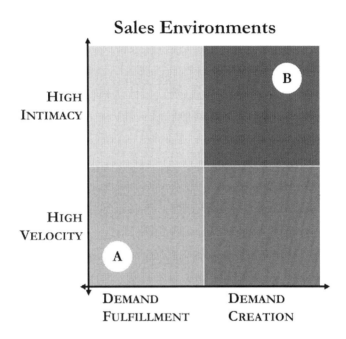

Different sales roles require different skills and even different DNA. First define the role, then pick the person.

Bill Polian (former GM of the Indianapolis Colts, Carolina Panthers and Buffalo Bills) had this to say about how Bill Walsh of the 49ers approached the problem: "We started talking about what people today call 'system fit'—how you fit players into a specific offensive and defensive system. He was the first coach I'd come across who had a really firm idea, right down to the last detail, about how he wanted to structure the squad—skill set, size." It matters.

Recipe for hiring salespeople who can sell

1. **Adopt a selling system** and standardize the company on it. This will establish a common language for the sales

process. It also makes selling less like black magic and more like a science.

2. **Be specific.** Identify the top behaviors required to succeed in the sales role for which you are hiring. Don't hire a "Business Development Manager" who thinks their job is to "create strategic partnerships," if what you really need is someone to prospect on the phone.

3. **To predict what they will do, find out what they have done.** Conduct a behavioral interview, requiring the candidate to prove to you they have done the behaviors that the position requires. Isolate the relevant pieces of data, ignore the rest. In the case of hiring, that means pick the three to five most important behaviors and then look for someone who has done those things.

   If you want someone who can sell in an entrepreneurial environment, pick someone who has had that experience. You need someone who has sold successfully without an established brand or demand. You also want someone who is willing to prospect, so if you can't find someone who has sold at a start-up, at least find someone who has been in a prospecting role.

4. **Don't settle.** Stay picky and be proactive. The good ones are somewhere being successful, and you have to go find them. In a recent round of hiring I went through 3,000 resumés to fill ten positions. If you settle for less, these bad hires will pull the whole team down to their level.

Sample sales interview questions

Key behavior: Use the phone to get appointments with superintendents or school board presidents in local school districts for a startup company.

140

Interview Questions:

- Have you ever sold at a startup?
- Have you ever had to do extensive prospecting?
- In which jobs?
- What were you selling?
- To whom?
- Did you use the phone, or walk in?
- Can you tell me how you do it? (Let them describe it and ask a few follow-up questions.)
- Let's role-play it. (People who can make cold calls can also role-play the process, because they are similar behaviors.)

If you put the right filter in place, only the best, most suitable candidates will get through. If you screen for the required behaviors, you will also ensure you don't pass on a good candidate.

Lead lemmings: A note on hiring a sales manager

I sat in on a sales meeting held by the president of a global company. The attendees were the sales VPs from around the world. When the VPs got to speak, they said things like:

- The competition is charging a lot less!
- We don't have enough engineers to do proofs of value!
- We don't have enough leads!
- Cash is tight!
- My territory is too small!

Their basic message was, "I am failing and it's not my fault!"

As long as the managers are leading the whining, there's little hope of a positive culture. These "C" managers will only attract "C" or "D" talent. "A" talent will leave an environment like this.

You can add that to the list of whines I heard that day; "Our top three reps left last year!"

These managers are weak and propagating their weaknesses across the team.

Steve Young, former quarterback of the San Francisco 49ers recalls that Bill Walsh and team owner Eddie DeBartolo "were both absolutely, completely, and utterly in agreement that the players were what mattered. In most of the league, the players were chattel. Eddie and Bill focused on them as the key principle pieces to the business. … That changes the nature of the NFL."

It changes the nature of any business.

9 TRAINING

Your Sales Team

| Manage |
| Coach |
| Train |
| People |
| Sales Force Structure |
| Selling System |

Training

Now having found the right person, and hired her for a defined role, you can train her on the best way to perform this role.

Or so it seems.

Earlier I told the story of an entrepreneurial CEO who shamelessly abdicated his role as a manager by claiming the job was Sales 101, and he could hire for that. It's something I feel strongly about. One simply doesn't abdicate leadership.

The impact of abdication

In an environment of management abdication, the selling function is a "black box." The sales process is opaque. You cannot inspect it, troubleshoot it, or improve it.

Sales managers and salespeople, in non-sales-driven cultures, conspire to maintain this "black box" status. It allows managers to avoid personal involvement in the aspects of selling they dislike. Salespeople like this environment of abdication because they avoid accountability.

The null set

You may be thinking, "I want to hire salespeople who don't need training or coaching. I want to hire senior talent."

Entrepreneurs are by nature impatient and want to cut through rather than untie the Gordian knot. The cry is heard through the hallways: "Hire the right person and give them a loose rein." Entrepreneurs make the assumption that the "right guy" is the solution.

> ### The Value of a People Person
>
> "The ability to deal with people is as purchasable a commodity as sugar or coffee and I will pay more for that ability than for any other under the sun."
>
> — John D. Rockefeller

John D. Rockefeller certainly believed you can hire sales talent. But he was also well aware that truly excellent salespeople understand how to deal with people.

The ability to deal with people may seem rather unremarkable, even pedestrian. But Rockefeller regarded it as a very rare quality indeed. In fact, in his eyes it was the most valuable commodity on earth.

Why?

Supply and demand.

The ability to sell is rare, and those who can do it are already somewhere being successful. There are not enough accomplished salespeople to fill all the open sales slots.

If you are the George Steinbrenner of sales teams, you may be able to buy a team.

But most hiring managers find that the intersection between those who can do it by themselves and those who are available is the null set (ø).

People who can succeed without help   **People who will take your sales job**

Deploying the selling system

The key to getting extraordinary performance from ordinary people is a system. As I edit this manuscript, I am staying at a Marriott. The property is an older one. I have friends who work for the company, and I happen to know that they do not pay expressly for talent. And yet they do get extraordinary performance from ordinary people.

I experience that every day that I'm here: The offer of a freshly-made smoothie while I eat breakfast; a cheerful hello from everyone I meet; a mixer and free beer for guests in the evening; a young boy spills a drink and the staff rushes to comfort him, refill his cup, and clean up the spill. They live the spirit to serve.

If you read *The Spirit to Serve Marriott's Way* by J.W. Marriott you will find this level of performance results from systems; systems for making hash browns to making a bed. Behind great performance is great process.

Successful deployment of your selling system will require that you fully understand and incorporate the following concepts into your plans and actions:

1. Visible support from the leadership team is central to successful change. Buy-in started back when you got the top sales thinkers in a room to help you design the process. Now that it's their baby they will support it. If they support it, others will follow their lead.

2. Unrelenting focus on the basics is imperative. True change takes dedicated time and focus.

3. Front line managers are the backbone of the system.

4. The system can and must be hardwired into processes your reps do anyway, like forecasting.

Sporadic or inconsistent training

Sales training fails if it's treated as an event rather than an ongoing process. The sales team cynically (and understandably) views it as the "corporate flavor of the month."

Training must be easily digestible. Instruction should be limited to small chunks. And you should give your salespeople a chance to try it in the field immediately. Implementation of a new process is always accompanied by a level of discomfort. Your salespeople may give it a the old college try, and if it doesn't feel right, they'll abandon it.

Your managers will need to provide continual support, reinforcement, encouragement, and incentives. And they'll need to hold their people accountable for applying what they've learned, mainly through the awkward transition until the new skills become natural and productive..

An ongoing program ensures that your salespeople move beyond mere knowledge to mastery. As a result, under pressure in a buyer/seller situation, your salesperson will be able to execute effectively. Anything else is a Band-Aid.

The Unlearning Curve

"The difficulty lies, not in the new ideas, but in escaping from the old ones ...."
— *John Maynard Keynes*

There are two kinds of unlearning that play into the stickiness—and thus the long-term value—of sales training, notably with regard to new and/or counterintuitive ideas. The first kind is positive and necessary for growth, and we tend to resist it mightily for understandable but wrong reasons. The second is degenerative and not conducive to success in improving sales performance. It is the natural consequence of entropy, and must be actively resisted.

Unlearning Type #1

The first kind of unlearning, the good one, requires a conscious decision to set aside what we think we know, and willingly consider a new frame of reference. It's a very difficult thing to do because our beliefs get in the way. Henry Petroski put it this way: "Technologists, like scientists [and salespeople, and almost everyone else I would add], tend to hold onto their theories until incontrovertible evidence, usually in the form of failures, convinces them to accept new paradigms."

The reason it is hard to reprogram ourselves is the self-reinforcing nature of beliefs. Actions are manifestations of our beliefs. It goes something like this:

1. **Belief:** *Our beliefs are our current programming.* Imagine, for example, that I believe I can't hold my own in a conversation with an authority figure.

2. **Response:** *Our beliefs, right or wrong, cause us to respond in certain ways in certain situations.* Because I believe that I can't hold my own with an authority figure, I cringe when I meet a CEO. The discomfort in the room is palpable.

3. **Result:** *The response impacts the outcome.* The CEO notices my discomfort, becomes uncomfortable himself, and responds negatively.

4. **Reinforcement:** *As a result, the original belief is reinforced.* Now I'm more certain than ever that I cannot hold my own with authority figures. It's a self-reinforcing death spiral, like the clang bird (it's a '70's thing; Google it).

If we are to benefit from sales training and improve over time, we must learn to embrace the right kind of unlearning (of incorrect beliefs and wrong assumptions), and power through the discomfort of letting go of what we "know" in order to achieve a new, higher level of understanding.

Futurist Alvin Toffler offered an apt insight on the subject: "The illiterate of the 21st Century will not be those who cannot read and write, but those who cannot learn, unlearn, and relearn."

To achieve ever increasing understanding over time you must pass through a period of unlearning untrue knowledge. It's hard, but will repay the effort. If you don't, your understanding will plateau and no amount of time or effort will prevent stagnation.

Unlearning Type #2

The second kind of unlearning, the bad one, requires no effort at all. It happens naturally. It is characterized by reverting.

Selling and negotiating have two components: an intellectual learning portion, and a skill portion. What gets used often sticks; what does not get used gets forgotten, or unlearned.

Training, without ongoing coaching, is like carrying water in a sieve. Salespeople get trained. Some actually try the new ideas. Often it doesn't work the first time, so they revert to old habits. Significant behavioral change is hard.

Be patient. It will take your average rep longer to learn than it took you. If you lose the love you lose the person.

What works is an ongoing, sustained training and coaching program. Don't give up. Old habits will seem reasonable and good. If you give in to them or allow your salespeople to give in to them, the training will be unlearned and any value will be lost.

How to get your team to do something new

I find that getting salespeople to try something they have not used before is a four step process:

1. Get out in the field with your salesperson and personally demonstrate it on a call or series of calls, so that a salesperson sees it in action. A salesperson may intellectually understand the concept, but could be uncomfortable actually trying it out with a client.

2. Set the expectation with your salesperson that they need to be using the concept as part of the standard selling process.

3. Reinforce the concept by pointing out frequently the role it has played in a successful sales cycle. Many salespeople, when presented with something new and innovative, will tend to let one of their peers take the risk and test drive it. If they hear good things they will go for it.

4. Use sales game film as the basis for your mastery process.

Do not only provide product/capability training

Most sales training is focused on the capabilities, features, and benefits of the seller's great solutions. The sales team then dutifully goes out and delivers the message, only to find that they have trouble keeping the attention of senior decision makers. Product/capability knowledge is important, but used the wrong way or at the wrong time it will kill a sale. Traditional feature and benefit selling is ineffective.

Training should include three major elements

Good sales training delivers a right understanding of the importance of "client knowledge" so your salespeople can hold effective conversations that help them climb the food chain of value.

- The Selling System
- Product/Capability Knowledge
- Customer Knowledge

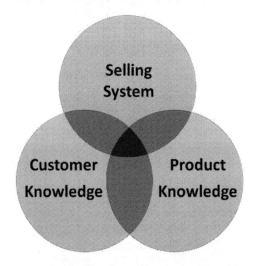

Training can be the point of departure for a new relationship between you and your salespeople; a conceptual shift from a reactive, "What are you going to close this month?" to proactive coaching in all phases of the process.

Early in this book I hinted that breakthroughs often happen by experiment and out of necessity. It's even true in training; and coaching for that matter.

As I've said before, practice is the key to skill improvement; continuous experimentation is the key to structural improvement. And it's good coaching that ties it all together into a package of overall performance improvement.

In the spring of 1954, Roger Bannister (at the time a young medical student at St. Mary's Hospital in London, and an amateur Olympic athlete) ran a mile in under four minutes. He had at last broken through what seemed to be a universal psychological barrier to accomplish the feat.

Two things about this story stand out as important for our purposes (apart from the fact that it's an astonishingly cool story).

First, because Bannister was a full-time medical student, he was forced to use a low-volume training regimen. After experimenting with several different options, he settled on a program that included 400-meter high-intensity interval training at nearly race speed. He also made a point of taking time off periodically to rest his body and mind. It worked.

Second, he listened to his coach, Franz Stampfl. On the day of the attempt to break the elusive 4-minute-mile), two teammates (Chris Chataway and Chris Brasher) ran with Bannister as "rabbits" to set his pace—following the strategy and instructions of the coach. Teams exist for a reason.

Conclusion

Performance breakthroughs often result from breakthroughs in training regimens and new training approaches.

10 COACHING SALESPEOPLE (CREATING SALES STARS)

Your Sales Team

```
         ┌──────────┐
         │  Manage  │
      ┌──┴──────────┴──┐
      │     Coach      │
   ┌──┴────────────────┴──┐
   │        Train         │
 ┌─┴──────────────────────┴─┐
 │         People           │
┌┴──────────────────────────┴┐
│    Sales Force Structure    │
├─────────────────────────────┤
│       Selling System        │
└─────────────────────────────┘
```

Coaching

Training offers knowledge and the initial experience of trying new skills through the use of role plays and exercises with professional feedback. Coaching ensures mastery of the new skills over time.

As I suggested in the previous chapter, training without ongoing coaching is like carrying water in a sieve. We train our salespeople and a month later they aren't doing any of the things they learned. So we tell them again in stronger terms, perhaps with a bit of bluster thrown in for good measure. Some of them do actually try the new ideas, but as I said, it often doesn't work the first time so they revert to old habits.

Significant behavioral change is hard.

Ineffective coaching

Suppose you hired a golf coach (just hoping for a few pointers to improve your game, for goodness' sake) and he told you, "The problem with your game is that the ball does not go in the hole early enough or often enough!"

You might ask for your money back.

As ridiculous as it sounds, sales leadership does the same thing much of the time. It's not uncommon to manage by outcome. Revenue, for example, is an outcome. It's also a lagging indicator. Once revenue is low there is nothing you can do. It's like someone asking General Custer at the Little Big Horn, "What's your plan now?"

A lot of sales managers don't add a lot of value because they don't really know how to add value. And in the vacuum, salespeople try to avoid them because "help" always seems to come in the form of lots of pressure. It's not actually helpful.

"Let princes not complain of the faults committed by the people subject to their authority, for they result entirely from their own negligence or bad example."

— *Niccolò Machiavelli*

Is leading a sales team different from managing other functional teams?

Someone once told me that that only a few professions require constant motivation. Athletes (and soldiers) and salespeople fall into this category. Leading a sales team is not very different from coaching a football team.

People tell me they got into sales because: "I'm a people person. I like people!" That may not be the best reason to get into sales. Most people who've been in sales for more than an hour would laugh at the notion that selling is a good place to get your emotional needs met. But there we are.

Selling is stressful. Salespeople are particularly vulnerable to burnout because:

- They place unusually high expectations on themselves.
- It's obvious when they don't meet their goals.
- They have a high need for social interaction, but they face a steady diet of rejection.
- Instead of supportive work groups, there is enormous pressure among their peers to win.

As a result, salespeople (like athletes and soldiers) are also quite vulnerable to emotional ups and downs.

Sales performance management is really less like managing and more like coaching athletes.

The whole person coaching model

When I was applying to West Point, I became familiar with the "whole person" concept. Applicants were judged not only on academics, but on athleticism, character, and leadership.

Great coaches coach the whole person. Optimum sales performance is driven by five dimensions of performance.

Morale

As with athletes, morale either drives competitive performance or undercuts the ability to compete.

In salespeople, morale is driven by how deeply and profoundly they feel about:

- Themselves (self-esteem)
- The company
- The opportunity

Beliefs

A person's current beliefs dictate the outcomes they will achieve.

Activity

Activity is about how a person uses time. Activity does not equate to productivity, especially in sales. Activity is productive if it is goal-focused and is driven by:

- A personal emotional sales goal, visualized
- A personal sales plan that is like a recipe calling for the proper quantity and quality of behaviors
- Behavior traps to drive goal-focused action

Ability

Ability is based on knowledge and it includes:

- Product/capability knowledge—Knowledge and understanding of my company's core competencies
- Customer insight—An in-depth understanding of my customer's world
- Mastery of a selling system

Style

In acts of persuasion, style trumps substance. I'm aware that's a controversial assertion. I shall explain myself presently.

Style is based on a person's

- Personal presence
- Vocal persona
- Interpersonal communications skills

The manager

Managers, as I mentioned, often focus on revenue, and it can be detrimental. Saying "We don't have enough business in our pipeline!" in an angry or bewildered tone *always* does more harm than good.

> *"A commander who appears bewildered in the face of the enemy will lose the confidence of his soldiers."* — The Leadership Secrets of Attila the Hun

Likewise, just measuring behavior (without regard to ability) can be counterproductive. Encouraging my team to make more calls without helping them make better calls is like encouraging them to dig a hole faster with a bowling ball.

If in the process of squeezing more performance out of my team I instill a sense of desperation, I negatively impact their morale and harm their ability to perform.

Too often managers act like scorekeepers talking about things that have already happened and can't be influenced.

> *"So much of what we call management consists in making it difficult for people to work."* — Peter Drucker

You cannot manage outcomes. You can only react.

Stop managing and add value!

The leader

A leader acts to influence while the outcome can still be influenced.

Leaders focus on their impact on the whole person, on all dimensions of optimum performance.

Leaders understand that you are always impacting morale, either on purpose or by accident.

Winston Churchill at the point when the Battle of Britain looked like it was lost said, "If the British Empire should last a thousand years, they will remember this as our finest hour."

At the time when they were at their lowest, Churchill didn't shout for them to fight harder or shoot straighter. He gave his people and his troops the uplift they needed.

In the worst times your primary thought must be to present confidence and to find a way, every day, to positively impact morale.

Leadership is a matter of having people look at you and gain confidence, seeing how you react. If you're in control, they're in control."
— Tom Landry, coach of the Dallas Cowboys

Developing ability: The sales whisperer

Entrepreneurial CEOs generally spend too much time on sales administration and not enough time developing salespeople. While it's hard to find someone who doesn't agree, it doesn't change.

What the CEO should be doing is:

- Pre-briefing sales calls
- Structured call debriefs
- Opportunity X-Rays
- Getting personally involved with large accounts at senior

levels

- Riding along on sales calls, observing, and giving detailed feedback using a known, standard checklist
- Selecting one key skill for every rep, and working with them to attain mastery
- Leading sales calls to teach reps how to do the hard things, like how to say "no" to a customer and still get the deal
- Making cold calls with their reps
- Reviewing activity
- Conducting annual territory planning and briefings
- Critiqued role-plays in which you play the sales role— lead by example
- Reviews of call recordings—like game film
- Review mutual action plan emails to customers
- Sales meetings that help your team make continual progress

Micro-managing

Why don't CEO's do these things?

A typical answer is, "I don't have time and I don't like to micro-manage."

Experience indicates that in the realm of selling this most often means: "I don't have a clue how to do it."

If you can't do it, you can't teach it.

I understand your hesitation.

I tell my sales reps I'll lead the first few calls and let them observe. That's a high-pressure thing to do.

I've been challenged, in sales training, to make a cold call in front of forty people. I was nervous the first time or two. But I know how to do it, I'm using our process, and it works. The reps learn best by watching me do it.

When I'm working with a group, there's often a heckler who challenges what I'm saying. Often, the heckler is one of the better salespeople. The best way to respond is to say, "Let's role-play it. You be the buyer, and let's see how I do." That feels pretty high-risk the first time or two.

These are all "sales leadership moments of truth." You can lead by example or you can wimp out.

When you wimp out you set an example too.

You'll do better than you think. If you have a well-conceived, state-of-the-art system, it will save you. If you lead by example you will have the power to change lives and the credibility to lead. You'll also find, as I did, that doing these things takes your personal skills to a new level, raising the bar for the whole organization.

I'm reminded of the words of an unknown Anglican Bishop found on a tomb in the crypts of Westminster Abbey:

"When I was young and free and my imagination had no limits, I dreamed of changing the world. As I grew older and wiser, I discovered the world would not change, so I shortened my sights somewhat and decided to change only my country.

But, it too, seemed immovable.

As I grew into my twilight years, in one last desperate attempt, I settled for changing only my family – those closest to me.

But, alas, they would have none of it.

And now as I lay on my deathbed, I suddenly realize:

If I had only changed myself first, then by example I would have changed my family. From their inspiration and encouragement, I would then have been able to better my country, and – who knows – I might even have changed the world."

Start with yourself.

Stop managing and start leading!

Impacting Behavior

Behavior is about how you use your time.

Everyone looks busy (or tries to), but not everyone is productive.

Activity can be impacted at three levels:

1. **Set a sales goal.** Goal-setting is a powerful leadership tool, but only when applied with an understanding of how the human brain works. Salespeople (and all of us) do what's important to them versus what their manager thinks they should be doing. Most sales goal-setting is based on what the company wants versus what the individual wants.

2. **Develop a plan.** Use your selling system to define the key performance indicators (KPIs) that lead to accomplishing the goal.

    A sales VP told me that his people could not properly project their business. I asked what efforts he had made to improve forecast accuracy.

    He said, "Last December I asked them all to commit to what they were going to close in the following 90 days." I asked if that worked. And he said, "No. They didn't make the number they had committed to, and these were their own numbers!"

    Trying to manage revenue is trying to manage the outcome. It's not managing. It's reacting.

    Further, it is blunt and destructive. You are asking the sales team to create the instrument of their own demise and then beating them with it. Again, lots of pressure and no value added.

Lesson: You can't manage outcomes. Instead use the selling system to break the goal into behaviors that you can manage.

3. **Establish a system to track the KPIs.** A marketing executive with no sales or sales management experience inherited the inside sales team. She said, "These college kids are hard to manage. During specific call campaigns, outbound call volume is up. Other times, outbound calls are down!"

Lesson: Specific goals with specific timeframes that you monitor produce results.

The coach's impact on morale

Any connoisseur of great sports movies (and anyone with a pulse who saw the movie *Miracle* about the gold medal men's hockey game between the USA and the USSR in the 1980 Winter Olympics at Lake Placid) knows for sure that morale matters. In the movie, coach Herb Brooks (played by Kurt Russell) delivers perhaps the greatest pregame locker room speech of all time. Okay, I can't help myself. Here it is:

Great moments are born from great opportunity.
And that's what you have here tonight, boys.
That's what you've earned here, tonight.
One game.
If we played 'em 10 times, they might win nine.
But not this game. Not tonight.
Tonight, we skate with 'em.
Tonight, we stay with 'em, and we shut them down because we can!

Tonight, we are the greatest hockey team in the world.
You were born to be hockey players—every one of ya.
And you were meant to be here tonight.
This is your time.
Their time—is done. It's over.
I'm sick and tired of hearin' about what a great hockey team the Soviets
have. Screw 'em!
This is your time!!

It worked. Spectacularly.

A very large part of triumph is in the mind. That's why the "motivational speaker" circuit is so crowded and yet so lucrative. And it's why the morale of a sales team cannot be safely ignored, underestimated, or left to chance. My own experience (and experimentation) suggests that morale may be the single most critical success factor in sales. If morale suffers, everything else (beliefs, activity, ability, and style) suffers in its wake. Once negative thinking is allowed to creep in and gain a foothold, dejection and defeat follow with it.

"Battles are lost more as a result of discouragement than casualties."
— *Frederick the Great*

Managers often tell me that they agree that attitude is key. But they also tell me that it's not coachable. "I hire people with good attitudes and fire them if they get a bad attitude."

I think they're in error. In fact, I think that's one of the chief differences between a leader and a manager: A leader knows better. Leaders understand that you are always impacting morale; either positively or negatively; either on purpose or by accident.

My experience at Camp Buckner

As a sophomore at West Point I was assigned to be a platoon leader during summer training at Camp Buckner, which was my first real leadership role. At night I found myself inspired. I had so many nocturnal ideas about how to make things go well that I began keeping 3x5 cards by my bunk so I could write down my thoughts as they occurred to me, usually as I was falling asleep. In the morning I'd make suggestions to my company commander.

One day our tactical officer visited and did a walk-through inspection. He walked through my platoon and stopped by one of the bunks. He said, "Where is the washcloth? It is supposed to be displayed right here!" I said, "No one I know owns a wash cloth." He said, "Make sure you have everyone buy one and display it here by Saturday inspection. I'll be back!"

At the end of the summer my company commander gave me my performance evaluation and it wasn't very good. He explained that at the beginning of the summer he thought I was great to work with, I seemed full of ideas. He said that at some point, early in the summer, the ideas completely stopped and I seemed to lose interest.

I realized at that moment that the conversation with the tactical officer had had an impact on me. I hadn't realized how fragile my own outlook was. That single conversation turned me off. Other people noticed it. It was like a candle being snuffed. It was as quick as the flick of a switch.

Four questions for a leader

1. Have you ever had a boss who turned you off in this way?

2. Have you ever had a boss, leader, or mentor who turned you on and got the best out of you?

3. How could a manager do something that *inadvertently* has an *unintended* negative impact?

4. Which is easier to do, turn someone off or turn them on?

As I've said, in times of adversity your primary thought must be to present confidence and to find a way, every day, to positively impact morale. But in times that are bountiful, you must keep your team from feeling complacent. Success hides defects.

It's all too easy to accidently have a negative impact on morale; to be a spiritual vampire instead of a leader. It's easier to turn someone off than to turn someone on, to snuff out a fire than to light a fire.

Most researchers into the subject agree that achieving peak morale (in any human endeavor) depends on maintaining the right balance of positive and negative feedback. The magic ratio is approximately 5:1. In other words, a great coach consciously provides about five positive, uplifting remarks to balance out one negative, critical remark. (Note that criticism is sometimes good and necessary, but it needs to be balanced by honest praise, and plenty of it.)

I suggest that prior to every meeting with a salesperson you honestly consider the individual's current emotional state. Never take morale for granted, and never leave it to chance.

Morale boosting requires positive, planned steps. Keep track of positive feedback about your salespeople from customers, or from upper management, or from peers, and share it freely and enthusiastically. Congratulate success effusively, both privately and publicly. Share good news. Offer a chocolate.

Think proactively about how to bring cheer to each individual salesperson, each time you meet with them. And do it.

The coach's impact on beliefs

All of us are constrained by our current beliefs. Beliefs are self-fulfilling.

Most of us are familiar with the old saying: "I'll believe it when I see it." Most of us have probably said it ourselves. And meant it. Unfortunately, it isn't mostly true. It may actually be more accurate to say, "I'll see it when I believe it." What we believe matters.

The fact is that in the matter of individual experience perception really is reality. In a fascinating TED talk, Beau Lotto asserts: "There's no inherent meaning in information. It's what we do with that information that matters."

Advances in brain science and neuroplasticity (and in a whole range of fields that touch on beliefs) are astonishing. This is not the right place and I am not the right guide to explore these things. What is important for our consideration, however, is that just because I believe something does not make it so as a matter of objective reality.

But it does massively impact my subjective experience. What I believe controls my behavior. And much of what I believe is neither true nor helpful. Thankfully, I can change my beliefs. But it takes hard work. And good guidance.

Your sales teams' sales skills are driven largely by their current mental map. That is to say, their actions are either supported or undermined by their beliefs. Beliefs (like luck, it turns out) can be self-fulfilling prophecies. If, for example, a salesperson firmly believes he has to discount to win, he will certainly yield to the slightest price pressure.

If you want your salespeople to act differently, you will need to help them identify incorrect, disabling beliefs and revise their mental map. It's not easy. Beliefs are often unconscious, hardwired perceptions of reality. Reprogramming is particularly difficult because, as we saw earlier, our perceptions of reality are self-reinforcing.

Here's a story that illustrates one of the most common disabling beliefs salespeople have:

I was asked to speak on negotiating at the Direct Marketing Association in Alexandria, Virginia. When I showed up to do the talk there was a much larger crowd than I'd expected. I was expecting salespeople. Fully half of the attendees were buyers. For a moment

I wasn't sure how to handle it, so I asked the salespeople to shout out the top factor that determines whether you win or lose a deal. Almost unanimously they picked price.

I then asked the buyers to give an example of something they buy. There were several suggestions, but I chose printing. It seemed a no-brainer. I said, "Printing is a commodity. Surely you just get three bids, then pick the lowest bidder. Right?" The buyers said no. Vociferously. I asked why they would pick anything other than the lowest bid. They all had solid reasons.

Then I asked one of the more senior buyers why salespeople thought price was the determining factor while the buyers all said it wasn't. She said, "Because that's what I want them to think!"

Salespeople firmly believe price is the real issue. Buyers know it rarely is.

That's just one example of many untruths or misconceptions that salespeople believe unquestioningly, setting aside all of the individual beliefs and cognitive biases that unconsciously set us up for failure.

The job of a leader is to help people see reality for what it is. And the best way for a CEO to change a belief is to lead by example, and demonstrate the truth.

The coach's impact on activity

The old injunction to "work smarter, not harder" may sound pretty hackneyed to the modern ear. We've all heard it far too often to allow it to penetrate our minds and excite our imaginations. But that's exactly what it did for the pioneers of workflow process  engineering who first heard it live at one of Allan "Mogy" Mogensen's Work Simplification Conferences back in the 1930s and '40s.

The principle is simple enough, but the execution requires some thought and a good deal of discipline. We've already seen that activity is really just about how a person spends time. It does not necessarily equate to productivity, especially in sales. Activity for activity's sake can be deadly poisonous in sales.

The trick is to understand the difference between productive activity and unproductive (or worse, counterproductive) activity. Stick with the former and avoid the latter like the plague, and you will have good success. For winning sales, you can't beat the right activity, for the right reason, at the right time.

Quality versus quantity

As I alluded to earlier, *quality* and *quantity* are often inversely related.

Unfortunately, sales managers do not always make the distinction. They sometimes operate on the mistaken assumption that more activity must equal more closed deals and thus more revenue. They seem to be particularly vulnerable to this vain imagination at the end of the quarter, when they tend to get reactive. They initiate a flurry of activity, pushing the sales team for more contact time, more outbound calls, more quotes, more demos, and more proposals. The results are often disappointing, because these activities impact quantity but not quality. And what's more, they often negatively impact quality. Under pressure, quality tends to suffer.

I suggest you pick points in the sales process where you can measure both quality and quantity, and work on impacting both. For example, it is far more effective to measure mutual action plans responded to by the customer than to measure the number of proposals produced and sent out.

Measure customer activity, not sales activity.

The rest of the story

When looking at call stats, it seems to me that the people who are doing well have figured out how to do it well and are motivated to do it more. They do more because they are motivated by the positive outcomes of their own behavior. If you go to these self-starters and try push them, what impact will it have? (I hope you see it's often a negative.)

Those who do it poorly avoid it, because they are de-motivated by their failure. They haven't figured it out, and may never without some help. Many of these folks won't succeed, even with help. When you push them, what happens? You get more bad behavior; more quantity with no improvement in quality. You may even *lower* the quality of their performance due to the pressure they feel, or the resentment they harbor. Again the impact is likely to be negative.

Quality of sales behavior is linked to ability and can be measured in a number of ways. Perhaps the most effective is recording sales phone calls and reviewing them with your reps. There is nothing like indisputable evidence for instruction. It's why football coaches review game film with the team.

Unfortunately, the purely objective and highly instructive use of call recordings is rarely done because it's time consuming. I promise you it's worth it. A good football coach would never dream of passing up the opportunity to review game film with his players because it takes too much time. A good football coach recognizes that it's an excellent use of time and makes it a top priority because it works.

Other effective ways to measure the quality of sales behavior include:

- Using an objective yardstick, like a sales debriefing checklist, based on your selling system.
- Riding along on sales calls, observing, and giving detailed feedback.

- Providing opportunity reviews using a standard, structured deal X-Ray format.
- Requiring customer-approved emails that recap all of the key agreements reached as the opportunity was qualified for all forecasted opportunities

The coach's impact on ability

In 2010, Washington Redskins' two-time All-Pro defensive linebacker Albert Haynesworth was suspended without pay because according to head coach Mike Shanahan he would simply not cooperate with the team's coaching staff.

The crux of the problem was that the Redskins switched from a 4-3 defense (within which Haynesworth had excelled for his entire career), to a 3-4 defense (within which he felt constrained to fill a hole, rather than create havoc). Haynesworth summed up the problem thus: "You don't have to force a round peg into a square hole."

In short, he had the skill set and temperament to excel in one set of conditions, but not in a different set of seemingly similar conditions. It happens all the time.

It is not uncommon for entrepreneurs—who tend to be impatient by nature—and even some senior sales leaders to eschew the hard work of building and developing a sales team and instead try to take a shortcut by just hiring senior salespeople. Like many shortcuts in life, it can be a costly error.

The rationale seems plausible on the face of it: If you hire the right set of seasoned sales talent you can just set them loose to plunder the vast pool of ready buyers who'll be mere putty in their experienced hands. And you can avoid all of the drudgery, expense, and occasional heartache of training and coaching a fresh crop of recruits. What could possibly go wrong?

There are some serious flaws in this kind of magical thinking. The first of course, is it begs the obvious question: If your salespeople are self-sufficient and need neither coaching nor training, why do you need a sales leader? The second is the simple fact that not all sales success is equal. A person can be extremely successful in one industry or environment working in a particular context or set of circumstances, and then fall flat on his face somewhere else when faced with a different set of challenges.

But the really difficult problem is the fact that the intersection between those who can do it by themselves and those who will work for you is, as we've already referenced, the null set. The ability to sell is rare, and those who can do it are already somewhere being successful.

To put it bluntly, there are no shortcuts in the formation of a sales team. Salespeople, like professional football players, must adapt to the system within which they are working. If the skills they bring to the table don't transfer to a particular job, they must acquire the needed skills through training and coaching.

The coach's impact on style

In 1960, the first televised presidential debate between John F. Kennedy and Richard M. Nixon revealed an important insight into the criticality of non-verbal communication. People who watched the debate on  television thought Kennedy won the debate decisively. People who heard the debate on the radio, by contrast, thought Nixon won—by an even wider margin.

I made a bold statement earlier that in matters of persuasion, style trumps substance. By style I mean charm, wit, and kindness. I do not mean to say that style is more important than substance, but that all other things being equal, style takes the trick.

There's a wonderful little story sometimes told of a Victorian lady that might serve to illustrate what I mean. After sitting next to British Prime Minister William Gladstone at a dinner, our heroine commented: "I thought he was the cleverest man in England. But when I sat next to Disraeli I thought I was the cleverest woman."

If two sellers are offering the same product with equal capabilities and equally good service at the same price, buyers will opt for the salesperson that they like, the one who makes them feel more comfortable, more understood.

It is proverbial that people buy from people they trust. The tipping point in a sale is often no more than a visceral response to another human. The emotional impact one person has on another is driven not so much by what they say (substance) but how they say it (style). If you don't believe me, look into the fascinating work of UCLA psychology professor Albert Mehrabian.

Words, for the most part, are under our conscious control. We try to select our words carefully; we moderate our phraseology. From an early age we are taught to self-edit. Not so with our body language. Most of us are only vaguely aware of the emotional power of nonverbal communication. We note how people make us feel, but we don't always wonder why. We weren't taught to. Consequently, our own body language remains unconscious and therefore unedited, uncontrolled, involuntary.

Left to chance, the majority of what we are communicating to our audience may not be what we hope (or intend) to communicate at all. We too often unconsciously broadcast our current, emotional condition. An intellectually perfect argument, for example, if presented by someone who lacks confidence, will likely fail.

Fortunately, while it is a sensitive and personal area, managers can impact style. And they should. Managers need to help salespeople cultivate habits of positive and effective human interactive behaviors, both verbal and non-verbal. There is a valuable body of literature on the subject precisely because it matters. And human interactive behavior is a skillset that can be learned, but only if we are aware of the fact. Absent direct conscious oversight, our brains act on autopilot.

The psychiatrist Carl Jung is widely quoted as having said: "Until we bring the unconscious to the conscious level, it will control our lives, and we will call it fate." Managers need to help salespeople recognize their behaviors and redirect them. It's not easy (because demeanor, appearance, and mannerisms are highly personal and therefore rather sensitive topics), but it is important.

Ride-alongs, role-plays, and game film provide excellent opportunities for managers to offer feedback to salespeople on how they are coming across, and why. Video and audio recordings especially can help people see themselves as others do. They tend to self-correct. Again, it's like watching game film for athletes.

11 MANAGING SALESPEOPLE

Your Sales Team

Managing

Selling is not a black art. But as long as leaders allow it to be viewed as some sort of magic, it will be unmanageable.

We have already noted that while coaching ensures mastery of a skill in the learning phase, managing ensures continuous application of the system by everyone.

New Leaders

I was an infantry platoon leader in the 82nd Airborne Division in 1981. In 2001, I finally realized what my job as a platoon leader had actually been. As a young lieutenant, I didn't have that clarity. It took me 20 years to really understand what that job had been.

It's really pretty simple. My job as a first line leader was to focus on the fundamentals; shoot, move, and communicate. The best first line leaders create a climate of continuous improvement by teaching and delivering feedback, and by making it fun and challenging.

New leaders in all roles may suffer the same confusion. A seasoned sales VP once told me, "When I first became a sales manager I thought everything I did was sales management, because that's what it said on my business card."

Sales management tools include:

- Sales meetings
- Sales forecasts
- Compensation plans
- Account and territory assignments

This chapter includes guidance for all of these sales leadership activities.

Suggested sales meeting agenda

Management Plan for a Great Sales Leader's Notebook

Daily
08:30- 08:45
Walk around. Everyone should be making the first dial.

08:45 – 09:30
Listen to random reps' calls and critique to a standard. Tell the reps in advance, "I draw a name from a hat every day. I expect you to have sixty names and numbers queued up and ready to dial."

13:00-13:45
Walk around. Everyone should be making the first dial of the second dedicated outbound call period.

Weekly
Sales Meeting
One Deal X-Ray per rep

Monthly
Review KPI's with each rep
Morale booster event

Quarterly
Performance reviews
A day of training

You can use the five points of the sales star model as the basis for planning and executing the best possible sales meeting.

Try to touch at least briefly on each of the points in your regular sales meetings. You can even use the points as the framework for your agenda.

Morale

Begin each meeting by attending to morale because it sets the right tone, and it matters enormously. Celebrate a success, share some good news about the company, or bring in an interesting outside speaker.

While we're on the subject of morale in the context of meetings, a word of caution. Have you ever been to a runaway meeting where someone starts to complain? If you allow it, the whole team chimes in and the theme of your meeting quickly deteriorates into: "I'm failing and it's not my fault."

Rather than letting the negativity start, use the agenda to let your team know these sales meetings are not the appropriate venue for airing grievances, griping, excuse-making, or other beefs. Let the team know that you can set aside time for them to ask for resources and to make suggestions, but that this is neither the time nor the place. In this meeting everyone should look to *themselves* and how they can improve.

> *"He that is good for making excuses is seldom good for anything else."*
> — *Benjamin Franklin*

Use your meetings to create a culture of continuous improvement, self-awareness, humility, and willingness to improve.

Beliefs

A sales meeting is an ideal place to uncover any current, self-limiting, or invalid beliefs that might be infecting the team, and to help your salespeople reprogram their thinking. Success propagates from your top talent. Your strongest team members will go out and try something new and achieve success. If you start the meeting with a success or two, it helps everyone else see what's possible. This idea is similar to the idea behind Montessori schools. Children learn better from other children who are a few years older than they do from adults.

Salespeople are more influenced by their successful peers than by the boss.

Activity

A weekly sales meeting is an opportunity to use peer pressure to enhance accountability. Like a Jenny Craig weigh-in, your reps are more likely to do what's needed if you make it public. Every member of the team should have KPIs that may include a goal for new calls, new contacts, new appointments, and mutual action plans (qualified pipeline) every week. Each of them should report their actual results each week.

If you are *consistently tough*, then it's less likely a crisis will occur and that more Draconian means will be needed.

When a manager tries to motivate a sales team by saying, "We need to find a way to move some of these deals into this quarter!" it translates to pressure. (It's a common misconception that adding an exclamation point to your tone of voice is motivational. It may have other than the intended effect. And anyway, such obvious and incessant massaging of the sales funnel is not unlike Tommy Boy petting his pet roll.)

Pressure from leadership to make the numbers results in management pressure on salespeople, which results in sales pressure on customers, who are not amused. The typical result if sales don't blow up is widespread discounting.

If you are going to apply pressure and require more activity from your salespeople, do it at the beginning of the month and focus on:

- Prospecting
- Digging deeper into dissatisfaction (by asking *all* of the ten questions recommended in the diagnostic checklist)
- Initiating and maintaining more senior relationships
- Getting stronger commitments from customers

And be sure your salespeople understand how to exert the right amount of energy on each deal, and just as importantly to know when enough is enough.

Ability

It's always fair for a manager to ask, "How did you push yourself this week?" Unless someone's perfect, there's an answer.

> *"My job as a coach is to make people do what they don't want to do, so they can be what they want to be." — Tom Landry*

Spend a little time in each sales meeting practicing one or two of the fundamentals of good selling. For example, you might role play developing a mutual agenda or practice asking the ten questions used

to diagnose a unique need. Or maybe critique a call recording, debrief a particular call you rode along on, or publicly review a specific opportunity.

These are all ways to accurately assess technique, pick areas for improvement, and then work toward the next level. I recommend the use of sales checklists, such as my Perfect Outbound Call checklist and my Perfect Discovery Call checklist.

Style

Not unlike actors, salespeople need good stage direction. Give very specific feedback not only on what to say, but also how to say it. Help your salespeople to practice effective personal presence, vocal persona, and interactive style.

General guidelines for sales meetings

- Do not pass out administrative things you could have done via email.

- Do not engage in deal-level discussions that go too in-depth on a particular rep's deal. A success case study—if it's done with training in mind—is a good idea. But the standard, "Jim, how is Monsanto going?" could and should be done in a one-on-one. This is *you* wasting reps' time.

Plan and execute a different kind of sales meeting and get a different result.

Why forecasts are inaccurate and how to fix the problem

Forecasting is an old problem, and it's not confined to sales.

During World War II, a group of Army officers led by economist Kenneth Arrow was assigned the task of forecasting the weather a month in advance. Concluding that their numbers were no better than those picked out of a hat, they asked to be relieved and reassigned. The reply they received said, "The commanding general is well aware that the forecasts are no good. However, he needs them for planning purposes."

Now let's translate that to sales. The forecast is no good, but we need it to run the company.

Despite tons of money spent on CRM software, and hours of time dedicated to business pipeline reviews, the forecast is still not accurate.

Why?

Hope-based forecasting

The fundamental flaw in all forecasting is that we are asking salespeople to report on their own performance. It's a bit like the US Congress asking pro baseball players if they use steroids. If we ask salespeople to report that they are failing, we are kidding ourselves.

On the other end of the spectrum, the top reps are probably sand-bagging.

Level-1 fix

Most organizations and sales managers ask for a forecast and apply a lot of pressure in the process. Recall the story of the sales VP who told me that his people could not properly project their business. I asked what he had tried to improve forecast accuracy. He said, "Last December I asked them all to commit to what they were going to close in the following 90 days." I asked if that approach worked and he said, "No. They didn't make the number they had committed to and these were their own numbers!"

Salespeople know you are asking them to create the instrument of their own demise. So the bad ones turn on the sunshine pump and the good ones sandbag.

You can't manage based on outcomes. If you want to change an outcome you have to address the underlying behaviors. When we beat them up with their own numbers, we aren't adding any value and we are probably damaging their self-esteem.

The result is a subjective and inaccurate forecast.

Uniform milestones and CRM

So then we try a "uniform milestone" grading scheme in an attempt to remove the subjectivity by establishing clear guidelines for what it means to be "at 80%." This is better, but still more subjective than objective. These approaches fail because they try to solve the problem with tons of paperwork or lots of annoying buttons in a CRM system. Reps gather all the information and then *put it in a file or a CRM system.* They look at it as busy work and they do just what it takes to keep their boss off their backs.

Sales compensation

Here are some ideas for a good sales compensation plan.

- **Keep the plan simple.** The more complex the comp plan, the easier it is to misunderstand or game, like the tax code.

- **Know the rules yourself.** Read the plan yourself, at least one night before your team does.

- **Make sure they know and understand the rules.** Hold a meeting to discuss it. Ask your people about it to check for understanding.

- **Compensation is role-specific.** Recall that when we discussed sales roles, some roles require a different compensation structure than others.

- **Keep it consistent.** While you will probably reserve the right to change the plan, try not to. If you find yourself tempted to fiddle with the comp plan, stop and consider whether you're fiddling with the right knob.

- **Good salespeople are in high demand.** Pay them well or lose them.

The comp plan should be a motivator, not a de-motivator.

12 STRATEGIC MARKETING

Your Company

And now, as promised in Chapter 1, we must take a look at the vital role strategic marketing will play in the success or failure of your selling system.

Strategic marketing is not strictly part of the sales team superstructure, but it certainly undergirds it.

While sales and marketing are of course technically separate functions, it is critical that they be seamlessly aligned, and in some places even integrated. If the sales and marketing functions in a company travel to the beat of a different drum, they cannot reasonably expect to reach the same destination, and certainly not at the same time. Strategic marketing cannot be safely ignored. Nor can it be taken for granted.

Incidentally, as with sales, market(ing) strategy is not the same as marketing tactics. In the next chapter we'll take a look at bridging the almost certain divide between sales and marketing, which will necessarily include some useful material on sales and marketing tactics. In this chapter, however, we will focus almost exclusively on the strategic aspect of marketing.

Strategic marketing

Both words in the term "strategic marketing" have essential meaning.

Strategic: If you are a for-profit company, your goal is profitability. You will spend more money acquiring your first customers than you will initially earn from your first customers. In *Crossing the Chasm,* Geoffrey Moore suggests achieving the "pin action" is the strategic goal of any for-profit business. It's a bowling analogy. When the ball (your sales and marketing efforts) knocks down the lead pins and those lead pins begin to knock down other pins (word of mouth), you get more revenue for your invested sales and marketing effort. Your full potential will only be achieved when this market-softening effect occurs.

The pin action is based on the self-referencing effect within vertical markets. This self-referencing effect is not obvious. It must be learned. This pin action doesn't occur by happenstance. It occurs only through focused intent.

Marketing: It all begins with a market. Markets are based on unmet needs. Achieving the self-referencing pin action starts by asking, "Who has an unmet need that we will fulfill?" Everything else about building your company is derived from the answer. We start with a market and then build a company to address that market.

By now you're probably wondering why you're listening to a sales guy talk about marketing. You might even be wondering why a sales consultant has an opinion about strategic marketing. The answer is easy. If this initial strategy is not in place, nothing I do will help.

Strategic marketing, not to be confused with marketing tactics

If you are having marketing discussions (about websites, collateral, logos, branding, and so on) prior to selecting a target market, you are putting the cart before the horse. These are all marketing tactics.

Here's why it's a good idea not to confuse the two: A marketing consultant suggested that a firm become a Microsoft Certified Gold partner. He suggested it was like a Good Housekeeping Seal of Approval. The customer pointed out that the certification requires a major expenditure of resources. Since the firm had not yet picked a target market, the customer rightfully suggested it was too early to decide on such investments. Further, he said, "If we decide to focus on hospitals, and the most prominent application in hospitals is EPIC, then it might make sense to become an EPIC partner."

Marketing tactics are derived from your market strategy, which starts with market selection. Once strategy is clearly defined, the right tactics will become apparent.

A firm that is pursuing an ISO certification, a Microsoft Gold Certification, and an Oracle certification, is a firm that will spend a lot of time and money in an unfocused way.

A company that is building a website with no target market focus is building an on-line brochure.

Tactics without strategy are the noise before defeat.
— Sun Tzu

Why the strategy matters, especially to a startup

Companies that *do not* start with strategy *do*:

- Start with insufficient capital to bring their offering to market
- Spend time and money in the wrong areas
- Continually switch focus
- Chase any deal that appears on the horizon
- Try to be all things to all people
- Choose the wrong channel to the market
- Employ the wrong sales approach
- Hire inexperienced marketing and salespeople
- Give them no direction or misdirection
- Fire them for non-performance

Can you be a marketing expert and a sales expert?

A marketing guru asked, "Are you a marketing expert or a sales expert?" Much of the world shares his view. Sales and marketing are two disciplines so different that one cannot be both. If someone at your company is not an expert in both, that will inevitably result in a gap in your revenue production, because no one can integrate the diverging marketing advice and sales advice. As the CEO, you need someone to make sure the marketing function is getting your team into the championship games, and making sure the stadium is full and the fans are in good spirits. If your sales and marketing systems do not mesh, it will be a serious problem.

Back to strategic marketing, not tactical marketing

It cannot be said too often: It all begins with a market. Markets are based on unmet needs.

Many companies are founded by someone who had a problem, devised a solution, and then offered that solution to others like himself. As an example, the paging device you get when you check into a restaurant was invented by two restaurant owners who were trying to solve the problem of managing seating at peak times.

There can be a market without a solution

A radio announcer remarked, "I put balm on poison ivy, not because it works, but because it itches so much I want to do something." The existence of a problem creates a willingness to spend time and money to solve the problem. When we have an unmet need we act. Even if the action does not solve the problem, we take action.

There cannot be a market without an unmet need

In contrast, where there is no unmet need, there is no possibility of self-sustaining, organic success. Markets are not determined by solutions. A better mouse trap will not sell if there is no problem to solve or significant advantage to be gained. Benefactors and taxpayers must fund activities for which there is no viable market—the arts, family farms, PBS, NPR.

Target market

Once a target market (a group of people with an unmet need) is defined, the answers to other questions can be considered. What services and products will we provide to meet the unmet need of this market? What is our place in the ecosystem of that market? What is the best channel to get to the market? What form should we take? What talent should we hire? How will we operate? How will we make money? How do we get started? How much start-up funding will be required? Can we bootstrap? What partnerships and certifications should we pursue? What products should we build or resell? These are all tactics and they flow from strategy.

But how do you go about it all? I recommend reading and using the comprehensive, step-by-step strategic marketing process outlined in *Crossing the Chasm*, because it will guide you in:

1. Selecting a viable market
2. Crystalizing strategy

3.   Creating a sales and marketing process with sufficient focus to ignite latent demand

The book is almost thirty years old.

Many people have pointed out that *Crossing the Chasm* was first published in 1991. Some excellent strategic marketing books have been published since, but nothing I have read has supplanted the guided thought process Geoffrey Moore developed. The current edition, as I write this, is the 3rd edition published in 2013.

Moore's ideas apply to products, not services

There are those who say *Crossing the Chasm* doesn't apply to services. Moore himself said the book was a niche book addressed to the esoteric challenges of marketing high-tech products. I'd guess he was employing his own principles, and knows full well that his ideas are more widely applicable. He's too smart to let the fungible nature of his work prevent its adoption, so he focused his message and targeted his market. As he points out, the concepts in *Crossing the Chasm* apply to products, services, and languages (like Esperanto), and standards (like the metric system). The original research that gave rise to the model was about adoption of new strains of seed potatoes by farmers.

Is it disruptive?

There are those who say Moore's ideas only apply to disruptive offerings. It is an unfortunate person who concludes that the bowling alley effect does not apply to their business. It is worth repeating that achieving "pin action" is the strategic goal of any for-profit business. This is true whether what you intend to offer is disruptive or not.

13 MIND THE GAP

The purpose of this chapter is to help you understand some of the difficulties you will need to overcome as you move forward with developing your sales team. It may seem at first glance a bit of a mish-mash of tactics, techniques, and procedures—for both sales and marketing—but there is method to the apparent madness. Approached from both sides, and melded together a bit, I hope you will see that many of the usual pitfalls can be avoided by a shared understanding between departments of what the other is trying to do, and why.

The job of the entrepreneurial CEO is to understand both sides, and ensure that where the departments meet they are aligned and complementary. The primary interface of course is with leads, which are necessary for the sales team to get onto the field and into the game, and which in many companies are supposed to be supplied by marketing.

Closing the sales and marketing divide

Almost every company you can think of, whether successful or just mediocre, has something in common with all the rest. There is a gap between the sales and marketing groups. In some cases it is more like a gaping wound, or a fathomless abyss. In others, who have worked really, really hard on the problem, it is just a small crack, maybe even just a scratch. But it's there.

Some companies try to bridge the gap by fiat. They simply put a VP of sales *and* marketing over both groups. And *voila!* Problem solved. While cross-training is a great idea, you are most likely to end up with a marketer in charge of sales or a seller in charge of marketing, either of which is like having a football coach in charge of a ballet troupe. Others make a genuine and serious effort to meet the problem at its source, and they fare far better than the others.

Regardless of how we face it (or don't), it is a fact of corporate life. Ignoring it will not make it go away.

Why it matters

In startup companies there is usually a struggle over where to spend scarce resources in order to get the company on stable ground as quickly and smoothly as possible. Is our money better spent on marketing or sales?

Because revenue comes from sales (and marketing is an expenditure with less clear ROI), sales often wins the initial round. And rightly so.

But if the company flounders, who do we blame? We know we have the best offering out there. The problem is that we do not have enough sales. So we fire the VP of sales.

And sadly, we may have the best solution. But, as we know, the best solution does not win. The best seller wins.

Traditional marketing may hurt more than it helps

The origin of classic marketing theory is mass-marketing via radio and television. Much of what has traditionally been practiced on Madison Avenue and taught in business schools is from those roots. Classically trained marketing experts view marketing as synonymous with "messaging"—advertising and brand awareness.

Rosser Reeves (on whom more shortly) had the brilliant idea of a unique selling proposition, and used it to sell a whole lot of headache medicine in the 1960s. When I hear people try to apply that idea to selling, it makes me cringe. If you have a direct sales force, there is no single silver bullet you can arm them with to sell your offering. If there was, you wouldn't need a sales force.

Selling is a two-way dialogue. It begins with deep diagnosis. In a consultative relationship, talking about "messaging" loses meaning.

Do you want your doctor to have "messaging" in mind when she sees you? She will more likely need to "un-message" you in areas where pharmaceutical ads have convinced you to be worried about myriad frightening maladies. Don't think "messaging." Think "diagnosing."

The inevitable gap between marketing and sales

A "messaging mindset" in marketing and a "diagnosing mindset" in sales results in the aforementioned gap between the marketing department and the sales department. While brand awareness and messaging are important, it is in lead generation that the mismatch results in problems. What marketing creates sales must be able to use. What marketing calls a lead, sales may view as a miss-lead.

You don't have to look far to see why the dissonance occurs. Take white papers, for example. Marketing efforts tend to depend on things like white paper downloads to generate leads.

Unfortunately, a white paper download may or may not have anything to do with a good lead from the sales perspective. If your salespeople need to enter accounts at senior levels, the white paper downloaders as a rule aren't the people you want them to talk to. And you certainly don't want them to start there.

Salespeople conspire to prolong this charade because:

- It produces activity.

- They are more comfortable talking to white paper downloaders than executives.

The whole process guides salespeople to do what they shouldn't, and detracts from the time they should instead be spending talking to senior people.

A friend of mine pointed out that many entrepreneurs will spend money they don't have on marketing before they will ever pick up the phone and make a sales call.

Marketing has its place, but it should never be done because it's the comfortable answer. Do what's effective versus what's comfortable. Selling is a contact sport.

Entry strategies

Value propositions and unique selling propositions are most likely to end—not start—a dialogue.

Here's why.

B.S. bingo

I was at a national sales meeting, and one of the product marketing people was giving a talk on the new version of a product. As I sat there, I noticed an odd dynamic in the room: everyone was listening with strange intensity.

I looked over the shoulder of one of the salespeople and saw she had a bingo card. She was covering the squares as the speaker used common marketing buzz-words. The sales team had a lottery set up, and the first one to shout "bingo" got the pot.

B.S. BINGO

Robust	Extensible	*Global Leader*
Best-of-breed	*Customer-centric*	**Enterprise-level**
ROI	**Strategic**	*Seamless*
Flexible	*Customizable*	**Scalable**
Win/win	**Integrate legacy data**	*TCO*

The gap becomes overlap

Lead generation is a point of overlap between sales and marketing. "Overlap" in many companies means they do it twice.

Marketing generates leads. The salespeople say, "The leads stink." So the sales department spends more time and money generating their own leads.

Overlap should be like the exchange where the baton is passed in a relay event.

The origin of the term "unique selling proposition" (USP)

Rosser Reeves (1910–1984) was an American advertising executive and early pioneer of television advertising. He was committed to making ads that were simple, direct, and often annoying (I can't swear he was actually committed to being annoying per se, but one wonders). His most typical ad was probably that for Anacin, a headache medicine. The ad was considered grating by almost all viewers, and yet it was remarkably effective, tripling the product's sales.

Reeves' ads were focused on what he called the unique selling proposition: the one reason the product was needed or was better than its competition. The USP was often a memorable slogan. In his words, "A unique selling proposition is a statement that addresses a specific benefit which cannot be claimed of any other product and which must compel sales."

In the 1960s, Reeves' techniques began to fail as consumers became savvier.

The goal of marketing is to tee up solid prospects for the sellers. Their job is to prepare fertile soil, if you will. To do that effectively, marketers really need to understand what sellers are facing. Here are a few basics to help align marketing and sales efforts.

The lowest level of selling

The lowest level of selling is represented by the salesperson who talks about his own company and its capabilities; he shows off a laundry list of products, processes, and people. He then hopes the buyer will go to the effort to make the mental translation from his list of offerings to their world and their needs. This is the salesperson who "pitches." Have PowerPoint, will travel.

In selling simple products and services, this translation is easy and obvious. Customers can do it for themselves. The USP was designed to sell very simple, low-cost, consumer products via broad-spectrum advertising.

A shot in the dark

Attempts to create a silver bullet for sales have the adverse effect of forcing salespeople to rely on a message that is abstract and non-specific to any particular customer. Don't forget that the USP was conceived for one-way communication. When we give salespeople a USP, they use it. Disastrously. If the only tool in the box is a hammer, most salespeople will dutifully go to customers and repeat it, hoping it will hit the nail on the head. It rarely does. In fact, it reduces the odds of success. It's a bit like playing the lottery.

If the USP doesn't convey value to a particular customer, then the conversation with that customer ends. Slogans won't sell complex solutions.

In selling more complex products and services, we can't expect the buyer to do the hard work of connecting our solutions to their world. The dream of conceiving a "one-size-fits-all" statement that will compel sales of complex, custom, business-to-business solutions is a pipe dream.

At the next level of selling, we invite dialogue and make the connection. Marketers can provide invaluable messaging assistance to help sellers make the general connection in particular verticals. But they need to understand what exactly the salesperson is (or should be) trying to do.

The highest level of selling makes a connection between strategic problems and aspirations (on which executives focus) and your capabilities.

Getting inside your customer's head

I recently spoke to a senior sales executive who was making cold calls to help launch another company. He's a sales turn-around guru, with many such successes. He said, "A good conversation starter is crafted so that the mere question indicates an inside knowledge of the buyer's world and lends instant credibility to the call."

Instead of coming across as paying a little attention to a lot of people, a salesperson needs to come across as paying a lot of attention to a few people. We need to take the raw material of features and benefits and fashion them into something useful for selling. We have to communicate:

- Insider understanding
- Impact

Marketers can help with the research necessary to develop impactful conversation starters.

Pitch the corporate pitch

It's always so disheartening to hear someone talking about unique selling propositions, value propositions, or the corporate pitch. It may be useful in tactical marketing, but it's never a good idea for a salesperson.

Consider these brave attempts to be relevant:

- The salesperson says, *"We have 40 offices around the world."*

  Will the customer think, *"Wow, a global leader?"* ... or instead, *"What a lot of overhead! Must be expensive!"*

- The salesperson says, *"We have the most extensible, customizable, and scalable technology."*

  The customer might think, *"So what? How does it help me?"* ... or maybe, *"Do these guys have a different dictionary than I do?"*

Telling your story leaves the job of connecting your capabilities to their needs up to your customers—or worse, *up to your competition.*

In other words, once again, the best product or service does not win. The best salesperson wins. And the best salesperson is the one who makes that connection.

Before you pitch, remember these important rules:

- Prospects become customers for their reasons, not your reasons.

- Your prospects love their own ideas and find them more persuasive than any idea you have.

- Your prospects will resist your ideas.

- Prospects seldom initially share the real reasons that they would want to buy from you.

- The real reasons that people buy might have nothing to do with the product.

- The real reasons that people buy always have more to do with feelings than with facts.

Understanding these rules separates effective salespeople from those who play the "pitch-and-pray" lottery. And a really savvy marketing department can help salespeople avoid pitfalls by knowing their own market.

A few principles of conversation openers

"The man who knows how will always have a job. The man who knows why will always be his boss. As to methods there may be a million and then some, but principles are few. The man who grasps principles can successfully select his own methods. The man who tries methods, ignoring principles, is sure to have trouble." — Ralph Waldo Emerson

Principle #1: Demonstrate versus assert

Robert Cialdini, in his book *Influence: The Psychology of Persuasion*, wondered "why it is that a request stated in a certain way will be rejected, while the same request that asks for the same favor in a slightly different fashion will be successful?"

One answer is what David Maister suggests in his book *Managing the Professional Services Firm*: that there is a difference between *demonstrating* and *asserting* your competence.

To illustrate the difference, consider the following:

"ABC, Inc. is a client-centric global leader with award-winning, best-of-breed solutions that are truly comprehensive in their scope of functionality; and we can help you integrate your legacy data."

versus

"When I speak with other VP's of retail banking, they say that cross-selling at the point of service is a key to customer retention. As a result of mergers, their customer information is in multiple systems, so that it is difficult for their staff to get the information needed. I don't presume, however, that you see that in your bank?"

If you assert your expertise, it repels people.

If you demonstrate expertise it will attract people.

Our first example is an assertion. Any assertion you make carries zero weight with the listener, and might antagonize her.

Our second example is an invitation to discuss the customer's problems. If you describe some experience that relates to her world, and draw out her knowledge, she is more likely to engage.

There is a natural force that drives most salespeople to assert. Fight it. Asserting, or pitching, is easier than initiating and sustaining an effective dialogue. But it doesn't work.

"If you have to tell someone you are a lady, you probably are not."

— Margaret Thatcher

Unsolicited advice is not necessarily helpful or appreciated. From the point of view of the buyer, if you start telling me how you can solve my problems before I have recognized or acknowledged a problem, you might be right. But you will not be viewed as helpful.

Principle #2: About the seller versus about the buyer

I was recently approached by a firm whose purpose was to make me feel comfortable referring them to my clients. Here are the titles of the first ten slides in the presentation they made to me, modified only to remove the company name:

1.   Our Corporate Overview

2. Our Senior Management Team
3. Our Promise to Our Clients
4. Our Offering Strategy
5. What Makes Us Different
6. Our Marquee Client List
7. Our Expertise
8. Our Three Business Units
9. Our Team of Experts
10. Our Value Proposition

If it's about you, your presentation is endured and forgotten.

If it's about you, your pitch drives your prospect to start making comparisons.

If it's about them—their problems and fixing them—then you engage them and help them take action.

Be about the customer. Always. It's the perfect place for sales and marketing to coalesce.

Principle #3: Your language versus the buyer's language

In the movie *Ocean's 13*, the team had a name for every con: The Gibson, the Ben Miller, etc. Once we become experts in our area, we begin to speak a new language. In the military it's acronyms. The problem is that we expect our customer to understand us. Abstractions are hard, if not impossible, to grasp. Specific stories and anecdotes communicate more clearly. Salespeople are like ambassadors: *effective* ambassadors learn the local language and customs to bridge the gap between cultures. Level two salespeople learn the language of their customers for the same reasons.

Principle #4: Broadcasting versus narrowcasting (revisited)

Finding and winning new opportunities requires precise messages to a targeted customer base. We have to ask, "Why would someone risk their job to put my products and services in place?" The impact has to be personal, emotional, and important or it will not motivate action.

Presenting your customers with a laundry list of your products and capabilities implies that you have no understanding of or interest in their business, and that *they'll* have to do the work required to make useful connections between their problems and your bag of offerings. Your value will be seen as low. If you walk in with a piece of literature or a canned presentation, you have reduced your value to the 75 cents it cost to print a brochure.

Increase the power of your content by focusing on your customers, their industry, their company, their major initiatives and challenges—in their language. The more you know your customers—their business, their system economics—the more you can add value.

Eight Ways Marketing can Help Salespeople Open Conversations

1. Take a customer-centered view by turning all features and benefits into an understanding of the *dissatisfaction* you can address; the current problem you solve, the anticipated problem you help them avoid, or the aspiration you help them achieve. Answer the questions: What is the problem we fix? Who has that problem?

2. Avoid geek-speak. Senior executives will send your salesperson to the person in their organization whom they sound most like. Companies do a great job of making sure their own individual salesperson is ejected from the executive suite and bounced back down to the basement. How? By filling them full of technical information and a language that is only spoken in the land of geeks. We don't teach them the language of the boardroom.

3. Plan to impact the salespeople's beliefs. We all find it easier to persuade when we are persuaded, so have customer successes and case studies play a central role in training. A happy and satisfied customer, a senior level decision-maker,

is the ultimate messenger.

4. Make sure the product training refers to the sales training you do for your team, so product training and sales training are mutually supportive and reinforcing versus contradictory. I suggest that your product marketing team, and anyone who prepares training materials and conducts training for the sales team should go through the sales training your salespeople go through. Product Managers who have attended my bootcamp have almost always remarked how useful it was to get a sales perceptive.

5. Include "anti-hype." Product marketing speakers in sales training sessions lose credibility with the audience because they sound like Pollyanna: "Everything is great and the competition can't touch us!" A more balanced approach carries more weight. I suggest having a module on "weaknesses, perceived problems, and ghosts from the past," in which a concerted effort is made to warn reps of tough spots they will hit when competing for business.

6. Give them selling tools and show them how to use them. Examples are case studies of successful sales, best practices, financial selling tools, five key questions to ask, etc.

7. Avoid "Death by PowerPoint." Keep slides to a minimum. They are usually a crutch for weak speakers. I suggest lots of interaction (Q&A, role-plays, a quiz at the end with awards) to keep it moving and keep them engaged.

8. The Best Messenger: Your top reps are thought leaders who impact your team emotionally as well as intellectually. Your team might hear from you so much they become "Mom Deaf"—so ask your top reps to share successes. Successful, experienced salespeople are effective messengers for a sales audience, and real-world stories of successfully closed deals are the best way to communicate to the sales team. Your marketing team could do part of the presentation and have a sales rep do a segment.

Lead Generation

Lead generation is at the point of convergence of selling systems and marketing. Below I will provide what I call the universal list of lead generation mechanisms and some advice.

First the advice

Step One: Review the universe of lead generation mechanisms below.

Step Two: Pick the top three for your business. Select based on effectiveness and not your personal comfort with a particular mechanism. Consider what stage your business is in. There are things you can do in the third year (referrals) that are not possible or limited in the first year.

Step Three: Learn everything you can about how to do the three you pick. You could spend a lifetime reinventing the wheel. Don't. Typically that means you need to hire an expert. There is a science behind each mechanism.

Step Four: Work the three methods intensely for a year. You will be ineffective at first, regardless of what you pick and how much help you get. Most folks do a thing, get poor results, abandon the effort, then rush down another path. Do it, measure it, fine-tune it, and track input and output.

Step Five: In one year, review your decision and revise as needed. I usually recommend that you keep the two best and throw out the worst. Pick a new one and keep experimenting.

Prospecting or lead generation methods (new customers)

- Referrals
  - From Customers
  - Referral ecosystem
- Articles—PR
- Seminars

- Reverse seminar—Invite a client executive to speak to your team/company
- "Newsletter" or email tips
- Google for trigger events
- Networking at their industry events
- Phone calls
- Direct mail
- Trade shows
- Ads—Web, print, radio, TV
- Placement in educational settings (à la SAS and EC)
- Speaking at industry events, or have customers speak at events
- Webinars
- Executive Events

Prospecting or lead generation methods (current customers)

- Referrals
  - From customers
  - Referral ecosystem
- Get invited to their meetings
- Call and ask for an appointment
- Project progress reports—upsell or expand
- Periodic management reviews
- Walk the halls at customer sites—keep an antenna up, find and develop dissatisfaction, suggest a meeting
- Senior partner visits with their executives
- Attend client industry meetings (network, speak, sponsor, clients as speakers)
- Articles (toot their horn)
- Team account planning (get everyone who has customer contact involved)
- Reverse seminars (they come to you and speak on trends in their industry, dealing with salespeople, etc.)
- Brown bag lunches
- Proprietary research/Monkey's paw

Nurture versus neglect

You want your salespeople to wear 90-day goggles. If they get a lead, they should decide whether it is worthy of pursuit now or not. It's a binary decision; yes or no.

However, just because a lead is not worthy of pursuit, you may not want to discard it. Your marketing mechanism should have a *nurture* mechanism that nurtures leads that are not ready and continues to develop them, without taking a salesperson's time.

At a minimum:

- Enter/update CRM
- Set a tickler for follow up
- Add to an email list to receive invitations or content that they will find useful.

Watch the pressure

Don't put too much pressure on marketing or your inside sales team to produce leads. Pressure will produce leads. But in the effort to get a lot of leads quickly, you almost always produce low-level leads. It takes more time, effort, expense, and creativity to get executive-level leads.

Pressure also often leads to low-quality leads. I worked with an outbound calling team and a young man named Alex. When his boss pushed him, he'd push customers. Most customers just hung up on him, but some set a meeting just to get him off the phone. These "put-off's" were the output of this process and became "leads" that were the input for the outside sales team's efforts. Few of the customers showed up for the meetings.

Too much pressure increases quantity of effort and makes reps push harder. But they lose finesse. Like a basketball player who tries too hard, he may get more rebounds, outrun the other team, and get open more. But he will miss the shot.

Once Alex relaxed, he quit pushing his customers, got into better conversations, and his leads became real leads.

Conclusion

Sales and marketing have a different focus and a different immediate objective, but they have the same purpose: To generate revenue (directly or indirectly) and make the company profitable. It is absolutely vital that the key point of interface be both efficient and effective. Sales needs good leads. Marketing needs to understand what good leads look like and to provide them.

14 CEO'S MASTER SALES LEADERSHIP CALENDAR

Initial activities (or first steps in a turn-around)

The CEO may get help with items, but must be personally, deeply involved:

- Review strategic positioning (see Chapter 12: Strategic Marketing)
- Develop and document a custom selling process for your team (see Chapter 4: Choosing and Customizing a Selling System)
  - o Derive Key Performance Indicators (KPIs) for each sales role based on the selling process
  - o Conduct initial training to kick off the process and to get your team's whole-hearted buy-in
- Review the sales force structure
- Assess sales infrastructure
- Review talent assessment and selection process
- Define a sales hiring process
- Review and enhance the sales compensation plan
- Review and enhance sales messaging

Annual activities

When you grow large enough to hire a very solid sales VP, the CEO may start to delegate this, but it's a great way to stay involved and sales-focused.

- Annual Sales Infrastructure Assessment: Review with the sales team the tools and systems required to support them and ask them to recommend any needed changes. The results are used to select priority projects for upgrades. You may choose to involve selected salespeople in action teams. Keep the sale team informed of progress to positively impact morale.
- Annual goal-setting: Each individual will set a sales goal, develop a plan to achieve the goal, define KPIs and then we will track performance against the plan on an ongoing basis.
- Conduct annual account and/or territory planning and briefings.

Quarterly, monthly, weekly, and daily activities

Once the system is up and running and smooth and level flight is achieved quarterly, monthly, weekly, and daily activities may be delegated to a sales VP, and eventually a group of first-line sales managers. All will have been trained and coached in the system and will have demonstrated mastery prior to this delegation.

Quarterly activities

- Conduct a full day of reinforcement or advanced training
- Update account and/or territory plans

Monthly activities

- Review KPIs with each rep
- Do a morale booster event
- Select one key skill for every rep, and work with them to attain mastery

Weekly activities

- Weekly meetings to support and reinforce the adoption of the selling system, continue building skills, review KPIs, and keep morale high
- One-on-one coaching and performance trouble-shooting

Daily activities

- Pre-briefing sales calls
- Structured call debriefs
- Deal X-Rays
- Get personally involved with large accounts at senior levels
- Ride along on sales calls, observing, and giving detailed feedback
- Lead sales calls to teach reps how to do the hard things, like how to say "no" to a customer and still get the deal
- Make cold calls with your reps
- Critiqued role-plays in which *you* play the sales role—lead by example
- Reviews of call recording
- Review customer-verified mutual action plans